D1361646

:: The Outrageous Promise ::

A STORY OF GOD'S LOVE BEYOND THE IRON CURTAIN

David M. Robinson
Gábor Grész

The Outrageous Promise

Copyright © 2010 by David M. Robinson and Gábor Grész

Published by Timóteus Társaság, Campus Crusade for Christ, Hungary
         Hungary 1116 Budapest, Zsurló u. 6.
         www.timoteus.hu

Printed in Hungary by Corvinus Publishers and Szekszárdi Ltd.

All proceeds from the sale of *The Outrageous Promise* will be invested in training opportunities for men and women in evangelism and disciple making.

Cover design: Gábor Grész

Library of Congress Cataloging-In-Publication Data (Hungary)

The Outrageous Promise

David M. Robinson and Gábor Grész

         Includes bibliographical references, appendix, and maps.

         ISBN: 978 963 87031 7 0

         1. Historical Non-fiction 2. Missions 3. Ministry 4. Leadership. I. Title

To God who "cuts through the bars of iron."

Psalm 107:16

"Praise the Lord! I will give thanks to the Lord with all my heart; in the company of the upright and in the assembly. Great are the works of the Lord. They are studied by all who delight in them. Splendid and majestic is His work. His righteousness endures forever. He has made His wonders to be remembered."

Psalm 111:1-4a; NASB

CONTENTS

Acknowledgements

Our hearts are full of thanksgiving to the Lord of the Harvest, whose faithfulness and enduring love are beyond comprehension.

With thanksgiving for their love, prayers, friendship, sacrificial giving and ministries of evangelism and discipleship, this book is dedicated to our parents, children, families, ministry teammates, ministry partners and churches—all beloved.

To our wives, Karen and Edina—your tender ways, amazing love, faithfulness, deep wisdom and enduring commitment keep us grounded, make the journey fun and make life profoundly satisfying!

Abbie, JB, Dan, Katie, Ráhel, Renátó, Gergő—words cannot be found to express the way we feel about you—you all make life so wonderful!

To mom and dad who love so faithfully and encourage so constantly!

Timóteus Társaság (Campus Crusade for Christ, Hungary) staff from 1989-2007—whose humble hearts and faithfulness to the Lord Jesus made 18 years in Hungary a huge blessing for our families and the best years of our lives ... so far.

Worldwide Student Network (Campus Crusade for Christ's sending agency for the Campus Ministry)—your commitment to partnerships changed Eastern Europe, Russia and the former communist block nations to the glory of God!

Dave English, Bud Hinkson, Larry Thompson, Ronnie Stevens, Mike Uno—friends, mentors and leaders whose faith, courage, sacrifices and wisdom made the difference!

Covenant Chapel, Kelenföldi Evangéliumi Gyülekezet and Rószakert Gyülekezet (our churches)—people whose faith and love give us joy on the journey and hope for a great future together.

Teri Chinery—assists and manages my sometimes crazy and always complex ministry calendar and found time to give two invaluable edits to this book, also.

To Bruce Neidenfeuhr, brother-in-law, friend and encourager and Ron Sterk, fellow elder at Covenant Chapel; both of whom spent many hours editing this book and giving us hope that it was worth writing.

Section One

:: FlashForward ::

:: Irony ::

(Budapest, Hungary 1997)

I n front of 450 colleagues, Éva was full of energy as she rose to speak.

"Twenty years ago, in this very lecture hall, I prepared to be a teacher and leader of the communist party in Hungary."

It was ironic to be meeting in the former headquarters for the Budapest Communist Party.[1] As Éva continued, she took irony to a new, mysterious level.

"At the symposium this weekend I have learned more than I did in the three years I studied here in this school. I will feed on this teaching for the next twenty years. So far in my teaching career I have taken Marx and Lenin to school. Now, I will go back and take Jesus to school."

As she said *"Jesus,"* Éva raised her hand to her mouth, her eyebrows shot up and she exclaimed, *"Oh. Is that okay? I am not a believer yet!"*

Gábor and I had our next newsletter. Another great work of Jesus was unfolding before our very eyes.

---

1. MSZMP Budapesti Székháza; a Villányi úti Konferencia Központ és Szabadegyetem

Thousands of educators in post-communist Hungary are characters in a wonderful story of God's love and power being told beyond the Iron Curtain.

It is a story of God's burden being shared with His people, envisioning them to live in glad surrender for His glory.

It is a story of God using unimaginably weak people to show others the enduring faithfulness of His love.

It is a story of the great works that God can accomplish through broken people of prayer.

And it is a story of people from two cultures merging to forge a friendship that would last forever.

:: Zdeněk ::

(Siófok, Hungary 1986)

The Robinson family was finally behind the Iron Curtain.

"We talk of the Second Coming; half the world has never heard of the first."

—Oswald J. Smith

We were a long way from home but wanted to be there. It was a dream-come-true for Karen and me. We were behind the Iron Curtain with our young family.

For years God had prepared us for the precious moments of 1986 at Lake Balaton in Hungary. We had been to Poland in 1981, and both Hungary and Romania in 1985. Yet, nothing like this had happened before.

Zdeněk (Zzden-yek) was intelligent. He was studying history and politics at a university in Prague. He spoke five languages: English, Italian, German, Hungarian and his mother tongue of Czech. He was from an influential family. His father was Director of Homicide in Prague's Police Department. He was sharp and in good shape, too. A starry-eyed Hungarian girl named Tünde clung to him as we spoke.

Something else was unique about him. Zdeněk was a communist who had never heard the name of Jesus before. He was an atheist-materialist raised on the doctrine of Marx and Engels. I had read about people who had never heard of Jesus. Now I was talking with one.

Zdeněk was polite, interested and humble. People who know other languages love talking with a native from a country that speaks one of the languages they know. Perhaps that was it. With eager intrigue, Zdeněk and I were engaged and enjoying a conversation about the Gospel.

As I shared about Jesus, it became increasingly clear that I had no idea that Zdeněk had no idea who Jesus was.

Referring to this man Jesus that I had been talking about, he asked, *"Where is he from?"* I thought it was a bit strange that a university student of his obvious intelligence did not know. I told him that Jesus was from Nazareth of Galilee in Israel. As I shared about Jesus' death, Zdeněk said, *"Oh, he's dead? When did he die?"* I told him, *"About 2,000 years ago."*

This surprised Zdeněk. He looked at me like I was a bit crazy.

"Why are you talking to me about a man who has been dead for over 2,000 years?" He studied history. It made no sense to him that he'd never heard of Jesus before.

I pressed on. I mentioned that Jesus' words and life had completely changed me. Zdeněk was both intrigued and confused.

"But he is dead. How can a dead man change your life?"

I said, *"Well, He's not really dead."*

Okay. I know you have to be smiling.

At this point in the conversation I did, too. Then the Lord broke through and gave me a great idea. I had to lift up the name of Jesus. I had to help Zdeněk immediately recognize the Lord's majesty.

"What is today's date?" I asked. He told me, *"June 20, 1986."*

I wrote Zdeněk's words on a piece of paper followed by "A. D." "June 20, 1986 A. D."

I asked him what A. D. stood for in Latin. He knew. *"Anno Domini"* was his reply. I asked him if he knew the meaning of Anno Domini. He did not.

"Zdeněk, Anno Domini means 'the year of our Lord.' The person we've been talking about—Jesus—is the "Lord" that marks our global calendars. Man thought so highly of Jesus that our history marks time by the year of His birth."

Zdeněk was mildly shocked. I mentioned to him gingerly that I thought it was strange that someone of his obvious intelligence had been robbed of this essential piece of history.

His demeanor was both humble and curious. We talked for a few hours and met again the next day. Although Zdeněk was not ready to receive Jesus as his Lord and Savior, he went away knowing about Jesus and longing to know more.

I was glad to finally be in a place in God's vast harvest fields where He had called me to go. Karen and I were talking to people who had never heard the Gospel before.

It was a dream-come-true.

But this dream began with a nightmare. Ten years earlier, as a junior at the University of Oklahoma in the fall 1976, God took me to a strange place for my tears to develop. In a dark and cramped place God shared His burden for Eastern Europe and Russia.

Section Two

:: The Change,
the Closet and the Call ::

:: Passion Is Lit ::

(Hopkins, Minnesota and Norman, Oklahoma 1974)

*"Here is a trustworthy saying that deserves full acceptance:
Christ Jesus came into the world to save sinners — of whom I
am the worst. But for that very reason I was shown mercy so
that in me, the worst of sinners, Christ Jesus might display his
unlimited patience as an example for those who would believe
on him and receive eternal life."*

—1 Timothy 1:15-17

I grew up in a great Christian home and went to church regularly. We had a very happy family life. I believed in God and in the main principles of Christianity. I went to Vacation Bible School. I attended Sunday School every Sunday morning and Royal Ambassadors every Sunday night. Yet in my teenage years, I walked whole-heartedly away from God and the Church.

I grew disillusioned. No one appeared better off in life simply because they were a Christian. It all seemed fake and a little shallow to me. So I quietly, almost unconsciously, decided to have nothing to do with Christianity any longer. It was 1971 and I was 15 years old.

I turned to three things to find happiness in my life: sports (baseball and soccer), girlfriends, and the party life (including smoking pot). Whenever boredom came, I would turn to one of these things to pick me up. After a while, I realized these things only distracted me from the emptiness that characterized my life. When the fun was over, the harsh suffocation of meaninglessness returned. Guilt and emptiness drove my life. I was living a life unlike the one I'd been raised to live. I was a black sheep. I knew it and felt bad.

On the outside no one would have noticed. I had great friends, did well in school, excelled in sports and dated cute girls. Yet when I was alone, I grew increasingly compelled to admit that something was wrong.

In 1974, during the winter of my senior year at Charles A. Lindbergh High School in Hopkins, Minnesota, I began to read the Bible and discuss it with friends. I began to talk to God for the first time in my life, too. But that is not all I was doing. My habit of pot-smoking was still very much a part of my life. As I read the Bible and prayed, I found myself asking God to take marijuana out of my life. It was hurting me and I knew it. After just four days of praying that prayer, God answered in an unusual way.

On a cold Friday night in February, I was smoking pot with two friends in a car. We were in an unlit part of Shady Oak Park. It was around 9:00 pm. We thought the darkness provided a secret place for our illegal fun. But out of nowhere, a police car's lights pierced the night as it roared toward us. All three of us were arrested for possession of marijuana. My dad had to come for me at the Minnetonka, Minnesota Police Station. As a minor, I would soon be called to appear in Juvenile Court. I was free to go home, if Dad agreed to take me. Otherwise, I'd spend the night in jail.

Facing my dad at the police station, I was not only embarrassed, but feelings of shame were dragging my spirit deeper into darkness. I was guilty. I was scared. Embarrassment, fear and shame gripped my heart. All of these emotions were going on inside me like a catfight when my dad came for me and agreed to take me home from the police station that night.

During the ride home from the police station, my dad asked, *"Was the marijuana you three got caught with tonight yours?"* I said, *"No!"* and then immediately started to apologize and lie. I lied telling him that it was the first time I'd even smoked marijuana! I added, *"I swear, Dad, I will never do it again!"*

Dad rather patiently said, *"Okay. I believe you. I'm glad you are telling me the truth."* This did not relieve me. In fact, I felt guilty for lying to such a good man like my father. Those were my thoughts as dad said, *"I believe you."*

While stewing in my guilt for smoking dope and lying to my dad, he went on to say that mom and my younger brother Rusty were crying as he left the house for the police station. He was trying to make a point. Dad stressed that if mom and Rusty were still crying when we arrived home that I should not *"misinterpret those tears."* Dad said, *"We are just confused, David. That is why we have cried. But they are not tears of shame. We love you. We will get through this. But you have to tell the truth."* He went on, *"David, when the Juvenile Court and police call us, you have to be ready. So let me ask one more time. Was the marijuana you got caught with yours?"* I immediately said that it was not.

I lied again. And I felt bad about it again. I was afraid of rejection. *"Dad, no! And I will never do it again. I promise! It was a mistake, but I would never buy this stuff. It was not mine!"* Dad believed me again and I felt terrible. I had used marijuana for three years.

When we arrived home, dad did not turn off the car. He wanted to talk a bit more. I remember the swirling steam from the engine going up against our yellow garage door, and looking out at the snow on the ground while we talked. Dad turned toward me and with a slight tear in his eye said, *"David, I have to ask you one last time. But before you answer, please listen to me. If you are lying about the marijuana not being yours, I think I know why."* I sat in silence. *"This is not going to affect our love for you in any way. Nothing you do will make us stop loving you. I just want you to tell the truth. We love you. Whatever you say, I will believe for the rest of my life. Now, was the marijuana yours?"*

I was stunned. I felt like God was in the car allowing me the freedom to tell the truth about my sin—to confess it all. I felt that dad somehow had separated me as a person from my bad performance and sin. I was loved completely—loved despite my sin. So, what did I do in that rare moment of grace?

I confessed. I told dad that I had smoked pot for three years. I told him that I had taken money from home to buy it. I told him that I wanted to change and that I was very sorry. I was free to rid myself of all the guilt I ever had. Dad's love provided a safe place for me to confess. That is how I felt. I also told dad something else. I told him that I was searching for a way out of my lifestyle and had prayed to God for the first time from my heart earlier that week. I had asked Him to help me get free from my sin, my lying, and be clean from all of my guilt.

Now I felt differently. Love and acceptance were demonstrated, making it easy for my contrite heart to issue an honest confession. The desire to turn away from my sinful life and wrongdoing seemed to flow effortlessly from my heart. God answered my prayer. God displayed His grace profoundly and personally to me through my dad. I will never ever forget that night because I was changed—completely.

I felt loved by God. I'd had enough of life on my own terms. I knew Jesus died for my sin and that I needed forgiveness. I turned to Jesus gratefully, knowing that He died to forgive me. He rose to give me a new life—a life I needed and wanted. I turned from my sin, placed my faith in Him, and something happened.

He changed me. Living in glad surrender to Him has been my joy ever since.

As I went off to the university a few months later my relationship with God was not perfect, but it was very real. Following Jesus was of the utmost importance to me. I longed to know Him better and for others to know Him, too. I went to the University of Oklahoma with a desire to see what God had in store for me.

I became a member of the Delta Tau Delta fraternity, got involved in Campus Crusade, played soccer for OU, and studied to become a Petroleum Land Manager.

In those years, my heart wrestled with many things. I remember the struggle to resist sexual temptation. I also had a hard time with my temper, which sometimes got me into fights during intramural flag football. I pushed through many a Sunday night to face another week of studies, work and a busy schedule. My witness in the Delt House was sometimes awful because of my pride. But more than anything, I wondered and often agonized over what God wanted me to do with my life.

In the fall of my junior year at Campus West Apartments on Lindsay Street in Norman, Oklahoma, God graciously allowed me to hear His voice.

It was in a closet.

:: The Closet ::

(Norman, OK 1976)

"When Christians in free countries win a soul for Christ, the new believer may become a member of a quietly living church. But when those in captive nations win someone, we know that he may have to go to prison and that his children may become orphans. The joy of having brought someone to Christ is always mixed with this feeling that there is a price that must be paid."

—Richard Wurmbrand, *Tortured For Christ*

In August of 1976, God had a burden He wanted to share with me. This burden was nightmarish at first. Only later did it become a cherished dream.

In between classes, soccer, intramurals and work, I would meet with five guys involved with Campus Crusade for Christ at OU. Bob Linn, the Campus Director, would bring material to our Bible Study that was filled with shocking stories.

These stories became the solid mist of a dream that God wanted me to pursue over time—stories that brought surprise and anguish deep to my soul.

Over a brief period of a few months, these stories that initially shocked me went from burdening my heart, to envisioning my soul for Eastern Europe and Russia.

The stories led to a serious investigation of *"the suffering church behind the Iron Curtain."* I read the writings of Brother Andrew, Georgi Vins and Richard Wurmbrand. I subscribed to a magazine called *Evangelism to Communist Lands*, the precursor to *Voice of the Martyrs*.

Everything I read brought tears. I was reading true accounts of incredible suffering. For example, one pastor was told to renounce Christ or else he'd witness his son being tortured to death. This man went practically crazy, but never turned his back on Christ. His son, just before he was executed, said, *"Don't turn your back on Jesus, Dad. It is not worth my life."* I read of pastors and their wives going to jail for their faith. I read of people losing their jobs or scholarships at the university for claiming to be believers. All of these stories were current, too. They were happening while I was going to class. People were suffering for Jesus while I fell asleep in church. People were being sent to prison while I was in Dallas for the OU-Texas football game. These stories rocked my suburban, fraternity world where everyone talked most often about Ralph Lauren and the Sooners.

Seriousness and sobriety were falling upon my sanguine, happy-go-lucky heart. It was difficult to sleep at times. These stories gave me nightmares. But I kept reading them. The more I read, the more I found myself asking God to relieve these people's suffering and bring about a spiritual awakening in the Soviet Block nations.

The small group that Bob led began praying for these nations weekly. Each night we would begin by reading a brief story of our brothers and sisters behind the Iron Curtain. Then, in order to identify with their suffering and secret underground meetings, Bob would make us get into a closet to pray for them.

It seemed kind of legalistic to me. At first, each time we got into that dark closet, I hoped no one in my fraternity would find out what we were doing. It seemed kind of hokey. That changed quickly.

I found myself challenged by the faith of so many who were willing to faithfully proclaim the Gospel and live for Jesus under such dreadful conditions. I soon found myself weeping over the tragedy of betrayal, beatings, executions and imprisonments. God was sharing His burden of love for this part of the world with me.

We prayed through strange passages from Bible for the people of Eastern Europe who were suffering for their faith—passages like Hebrews 10:32-39. We prayed they would continue to *"endure a great conflict of sufferings,"* to be able to *"accept joyfully the seizure of their property"* and not to *"throw away their confidence in the Lord."* All of this was new and even a bit strange to me at first, but God would not allow the burden to lift from my heart. Imagine a fraternity guy who danced at parties on the weekend praying that the people suffering behind the Iron Curtain would *"bear up under sorrows when suffering unjustly."*[1]

I could not get the people from these stories off my mind. Over time, I found myself burdened to the point of praying for nations and people from Albania, Hungary, Russia, Ukraine, Poland, Romania and the entire Soviet Block. I bought a world map and placed pictures and verses on it to help me focus and stay motivated to pray.

God was changing my heart. I became convinced that the deepest needs of the human race can only be met through a personal relationship with Jesus Christ. In my junior year at OU, I experienced an increasing desire to do something about meeting that need in Eastern Europe.

---

1. 1 Peter 2:29

:: The Call ::

(1976 - 1978)

"It has always been my ambition to preach the gospel where Christ was not known, so that I would not be building on someone else's foundation."

—Romans 15:20

I was not prepared for what happened next. I went to Kansas City, Missouri to hear a man speak who "ministered behind the Iron Curtain." Bud Hinkson was then the Director of Affairs for Campus Crusade for Christ in Eastern Europe and the Soviet Union. His fiery vision, joyful Bible teaching and amazing faith both challenged and inspired me.

As I met with Bud that weekend, God used him to plant the seed of desire in me to one day live as a missionary in Eastern Europe.

Over the course of my junior year at OU, the Lord led me to live differently and to make decisions that helped prepare me for the mission field. Outside of learning to love the Word of God, two decisions made a huge difference in my life. The first, a relationship with a young woman ended—our passions and pursuits were just too different. The second, I turned down a summer job with

Conoco Oil Company to go on a summer mission project with Campus Crusade to Myrtle Beach, South Carolina.

I met a woman named Karen Swiney on the first day of the project. May 24, 1977 was a day I'd never forget. That summer our hearts were knit together. That fall our love was declared to each other. The following summer we exchanged our vows and were married.

Karen's call to missions was more general than mine, but her convictions were strong and grounded in an eternal perspective. On our first date in Myrtle Beach I asked her what her purpose in life was. I didn't know it at the time, but she quoted the one who led her to Christ through his writings, Jim Elliott. *"David, there are only two things that will last forever, God's Word and the souls of men. I am going to have something to do with both."* Not only was she great looking, sweet and other-centered, Karen had the heart of the Lion of Judah beating deep in her soul.

While dating, as I shared my burden for Eastern Europe, God gave Karen a heart to pray for that part of the world, too. As we were engaged to be married, we decided to apply for the staff of Campus Crusade for Christ, convinced that we were called to minister full-time, as soon as possible, somewhere in Eastern Europe or Russia.

Little did we know then, but we would have to wait eleven years before actually moving to that part of the world.

Section Three

:: **Waiting** ::

:: Waiting and Failing ::

(Poland 1981)

"The heart is deceitful above all things, and
desperately sick; who can understand it?"

—Jeremiah 17:9

We served with Crusade first on the campus of Southwest Missouri State University in Springfield, Missouri from 1978-1983.

We strongly considered an international assignment with Crusade in both 1980 and 1987. We badly wanted to move to the land of our dreams—the land of God's calling. Yet, God had us wait. Looking back, God was building patience, prayer and ministry experience into our lives. From 1978 to 1989, God set us on a journey to prepare us for a future of incredible blessing, revival and spiritual awakening. We served in the U.S. Campus Ministry and went on short-term mission projects to Poland, Romania and Hungary during those years.

During this time, it felt like the Great Commission[1] and our calling to Eastern Europe was on a train moving quickly past us. We wanted to be on that train.

Waiting was hard.

---

1. Matthew 28:18-20

Waiting on the Lord and seeking Him in prayer must be deeply valued by anyone who commits him or herself to helping fulfill the Great Commission. God is not in a hurry to fulfill the Great Commission. Urgency should never be allowed to take the place of preparation. God does not seem interested in those who zealously pursue His cause, if they are not people of prayer and faith. His work is too important. To represent Him, we must be yielded, entirely yielded. Graciously, He told us time and time again that our lives were in His hands and we were on that train. He told us that waiting, praying and preparing are as much a part of the Great Commission as leading people to Christ and building them in their faith. Our time to move to Eastern Europe would come, but for now, we had to wait.

God kept our vision alive, despite circumstances that seemed to deny we would ever wind up living in Eastern Europe. In 1981, God gave us the opportunity to finally do ministry there. And, oddly enough, He used disappointment and personal failure during a short-term project to prepare us for a long-term assignment in Eastern Europe. In the summer of 1981 Karen and I went to Poland on a summer mission project. That was the summer when the Solidarity Movement (Solidarność), led by Lech Wałęsa, was at its strongest in Poland.

Before having children we wanted to minister in an Eastern European country to put legs to our prayers and experience to our vision. It was a summer of both joy and disappointment. The Americans and Poles that we worked with were incredibly faithful, a joy to be around and effective in ministry. We shared Christ, trained Christian volunteers and showed the JESUS Film all summer long.

Even under communism, the Catholic Church was very influential in Poland, especially through a man simply known to us that summer as "Father B." That was his codename to help protect his identity from the communist regime. Father B led an evangelical youth movement within the Catholic Church called the "Light and Life Movement." This movement did a great job of sharing the

Gospel and following up thousands of young people. They used the JESUS Film relentlessly, along with the *Transferable Concepts* by Bill Bright.

It may sound strange, but in some ways it was a disappointing summer. The years preceding Poland were dominated by thoughts, convictions and passions that God wanted us to go to a part of the communist world where the Gospel was not known. God's call to us was from Romans 15:15-21 which says,

> *"But I have written very boldly to you on some points so as to remind you again, because of the grace that was given me from God, to be a minister of Christ Jesus to the Gentiles, ministering as a priest the gospel of God, so that my offering of the Gentiles may become acceptable, sanctified by the Holy Spirit. Therefore in Christ Jesus I have found reason for boasting in things pertaining to God. For I will not presume to speak of anything except what Christ has accomplished through me, resulting in the obedience of the Gentiles by word and deed, in the power of signs and wonders, in the power of the Spirit; so that from Jerusalem and round about as far as Illyricum I have fully preached the gospel of Christ. And thus I aspired to preach the gospel, not where Christ was already named, so that I would not build on another man's foundation; but as it is written, they who had no news of Him shall see, and they who have not heard shall understand."*

Although the "Light and Life Movement" in Poland was an awesome work of God, we were disappointed that after five years of prayer and waiting, the first experience in the Eastern Block was very different than we expected.

The greatest disappointment in Poland, however, was my personal failure. Karen was a champ, but I was not. I complained every day in Poland. Oh, I did it cleverly. I hid how I really felt. Although I was my normal gregarious self, I laughed and taunted other Americans about one topic that represented my greatest temptation and desire—food. As I drank polluted water and ate fly contaminated sandwiches with lard all summer long, I'd say to the other

Americans rather enthusiastically, *"Man, this cheeseburger sure tastes good. And this Dr. Pepper...Whoa!"* We'd laugh. But deep down, I was complaining. I could not get food off of my mind. I lost 19 pounds that summer in a five week period of time.

We were there to share Jesus with these dear people. We were there as God's ambassadors to allow Him to entreat through us *"be reconciled to God!"*[2] Despite this high calling, despite this rare privilege, despite the fact that most people around us had never heard a clear presentation of the Gospel, my mind would wander to food far too often. One day our translator Dorottya turned to me and said, *"You Americans sure talk a lot about food."*

This hurt. I had failed. I remember weeping about that one sentence from Dorrotya's heart many times. I came all the way to Poland to talk about Jesus, yet my selfish heart was preoccupied with food. That is what stood out to Dorottya.

God used it though. He graciously burdened my heart beyond the barbed wire of the communist Iron Curtain. He went straight to the bars of iron in my own heart. He graciously rebuked me, went to work and broke through. I never felt condemned by God in my failure, just corrected.

I needed it, too. This failure caused me to spend more time with God, both in confessing my sin, learning to walk in the Spirit and asking Him to build my character so I could one day qualify to be a missionary in the lands to which He was calling us.

---

2. 2 Corinthians 5:20

:: Waiting and Darkness ::

(Springfield, MO 1983)

"I will lead the blind by a way they do not know..."

—Isaiah 42:16

We continued to wait. After our disappointment in Poland, God had one more character building test for us.

The summer months of 1982 were wonderful. We became new parents. Our daughter Abigail was born in July, but the joy of having a new baby in our home was interrupted quickly. A mere two months after Abbie's birth, both Karen and I came down with spinal meningitis.

That illness silently prophesied that it was going to be a difficult year.

In January of 1983 the lights went out. I struggled with leadership decisions, theological questions, and with trying to love people through very difficult, personal issues. That year, the Lord led us through a variety of circumstances that can only be described as hellish darkness. Here is a short list of what is known as "The Darkness of '83" to Karen and me:

:: We housed a suicidal student who struggled with homosexuality for about one month that year.

:: A cult from Boston started teaching a false gospel on our campus in Springfield. I spent hours and hours debating these false teachers polemically, helping students discern the truth and worrying about who would fall away next.

:: I personally doubted many things including my calling and what I believed.

:: We had our personal savings stolen during the summer. It wasn't much, but it was all we had: $3,500.

My world was rocking and my confidence was fading.

But God graciously spoke. If my life was a coat, that year I literally hung my entire life on the coat rack of Isaiah 42. It gave me strength and hope.

"I am the Lord, I have called you in righteousness, I will also hold you by the hand and watch over you, and I will appoint you as a covenant to the people, as a light to the nations, to open blind eyes, to bring out prisoners from the dungeon and those who dwell in darkness from the prison. I am the Lord, that is My name; I will not give My glory to another, nor My praise to graven images. Behold, the former things have come to pass. Now I declare new things; before they spring forth I proclaim them to you."

"I have kept silent for a long time; I have kept still and restrained Myself. Now like a woman in labor I will groan, I will both gasp and pant. I will lay waste the mountains and hills, and wither all their vegetation; I will make the rivers into coastlands and dry up the ponds. I will lead the blind by a way they do not know; in paths they do not know I will guide them. I will make darkness into light before them and rugged places into plains. These are the things I will do, and I will not leave them undone. They will be turned back and be utterly put to shame, who trust in idols, who say to molten images, 'You are our gods.' Hear, you deaf! And look, you blind, that you may see. Who is blind but My servant, or so deaf as My messenger whom I send? Who is so blind as

he that is at peace with Me, or so blind as the servant of the Lord? You have seen many things, but you do not observe them; your ears are open, but none hears." [3]

The Lord assured me that all our darkness was light to Him. He could see everything we were going through and was committed to guiding us faithfully. He was worthy of our trust, even when our feelings were gone. The Lord told me to keep doing two things, despite having a profound lack of emotional love for Him during this time of darkness.

1. Hold My Hand ::

One thing He told me was to keep holding His hand—that meant to trust Him. That is not easy to do when your emotions tell you that God is coming at you with a knife. That is how I felt. As Job said, *"Even though He slay me, yet will I trust Him."*

Over and over God told me that my feelings were lying to me. In Isaiah 42 God assured me that His hands weren't grasping an instrument to torture me, but instead were grasping my own hands in order to lead me forward—out of the darkness. God wanted me to know He loved me, would protect me and get me through everything.

2. Keep Walking ::

The other thing He told me was to keep walking ahead—that meant to keep obeying Him. A thought overwhelmed me during this time of great difficulty: *"It can get worse. If you stop trusting and obeying, then guilt and regret will be added to your misery."*

:: Hope in the Darkness ::

The Lord gave me hope, too. During those dark days, I'd go back to Isaiah 42 and cling to the hope these verses brought me.

---

3. Isaiah 42:6-9, 14-20

Hope is intimately linked to faith. You cannot have one without the other. Hope is the emotion of faith. It is the emotional life inside a promise. Hope brings the promise to life in the one believing it. For example, when my son Dan was younger, we loved to play baseball together. Each time I promised Dan that we'd play baseball the coming weekend, good feelings always resulted. Hope has a promise you can rejoice in! My promise to play gave Dan hope. Dan's hope to play baseball with me made him feel good. Bobb Biehl says that hope is *"encouragement for the future."* I like that. Hope's opposite, however, is despair. Both are emotions—hope coming from faith, and despair coming from doubt. We experience fear when we fail to hear the promises of God and when we fail to acknowledge His presence. A bad outlook invariably captures us, when we unconsciously and passively forget to welcome the promises of God in our heart.

I served as Campus Director at Southwest Missouri State University from 1980-1983. The year of darkness began in January 1983, my last year as a young director. Days became weeks and weeks became months. The shadows became thick clouds of despair. We made a difficult decision to leave the U.S. Campus Ministry and prepare for Eastern Europe in a new way. We thought it was best to go to seminary. We wanted to keep moving forward even though moving was hard to do. The Lord led us to attend Southwestern Baptist Theological Seminary in Fort Worth, Texas, while remaining on staff with Campus Crusade. Karen and I, along with our one-year old daughter Abbie, moved to Fort Worth in the summer of 1983.

As we continued to wait, God fulfilled His promise to us in Isaiah 42—He *"made darkness light before us."* The more we focused on His word and the promises of Isaiah 42, our hearts began to hope. Slowly, over the course of 1983, hope grew as we trusted God to do what He promised.

Our God has a voice. He speaks to us through His Word.

It was while at seminary, that God broke through the darkness. During the spring of 1984, our hearts for the campus ministry in the USA began to pound again. Our passion grew. We wanted to help raise-up spiritual leaders who could go to the ends of the earth. Healthy campus ministries that could send such laborers became our focus. So, after prayer and counsel, we accepted a challenge to go back to the campus ministry and leave the seminary.

I was appointed Area Campus Director for Kansas-Missouri-Nebraska. During the summer of 1984 we moved from Fort Worth to Kansas City.

The darkness had lifted, but it seemed that Eastern Europe and Russia would still have to wait.

Section Four

:: Burden-Vision-Responsibility ::

:: The Burden ::

(KS-MO-NE 1984 - 1985)

*"When I heard these things, I sat down and wept. For some days
I mourned and fasted and prayed before the God of heaven."*

—Nehemiah 1:4

As a new Area Director, in the fall of 1984, I began to visit all of the campuses I oversaw and the staff I served. I went to places like Kansas State University, the universities of Nebraska, Missouri and Kansas, Northeast Missouri State University,[1] Emporia State University, Fort Hayes State University, Kearney State College, and the one from which Karen graduated and I served as a Campus Director, Southwest Missouri State University.[2]

I met with full-time Crusade staff and student leaders, church leaders and supporters. Our staff really stood out to me. They led spiritually. They reached out to others with heart, skill and creativity. They were passionate. They had a vision for the world. Karen and I loved their fellowship and loved serving beside them. Together, we eagerly talked about the needs in the world and encouraged students to wrestle with the idea of serving as lifetime missionaries. The world

1. now known as Truman State
2. now known as Missouri State

and having a "vision for the world" were themes on everybody's mind. Praying for the nations was authentic, heart-felt and typical everywhere we went.

We encouraged everyone to read certain books that mentored, envisioned and fanned the flame for world missions. Almost everyone was reading and discussing books like *In the Shadow of the Almighty* (Elisabeth Elliott's edit of Jim Elliott's journals), *In the Gap* by David Bryant, *Operation World* by Patrick D. Johnstone, *These Strange Ashes* by Elisabeth Elliott, *A Distant Grief* by Kefa Sempangi, *Journey to the Nations* by The Caleb Project, *Perspectives* (the global missions course), and *The Master Plan of Evangelism* by Robert Coleman. Everyone had a world map and subscribed to mission journals. Publications like *Mission Frontiers* by Dr. Ralph D. Winter put fire in our bones.

We challenged everyone to develop a *"Great Commission Theology"* and to reside on this planet as aliens that belong to the Kingdom of God. Prayer for the nations grew. Vision for the nations impassioned every conversation.

Dan Hayes, a Regional Director of Crusade back then, once said that a revival is best described as *"renewed zeal to obey God."* That zeal was alive in hundreds of university students and staff.

But all of this effort and emphasis lacked something. It lacked real, qualified, mobilized manpower that actually went to the world—that actually took personal responsibility to go.

It was troubling.

We had people of faith and vision. We had 70 full-time staff in KS-MO-NE and about 1,200 students in small groups. We had Bible studies called Discovery Groups establishing students in their faith. We had Training Groups for equipping students in discipleship, Bible Study and strategic evangelism ministry. We had groups to develop and entrust leadership called Action Groups, too.

We even had a national campus movement, and with it the nationwide resources of Campus Crusade for Christ. Our national leadership promoted

"Stop-Out." Stop-Out was a program encouraging some to stop in the middle of their university career and opt out by going to serve internationally for one year. The U.S. Campus Ministry had an excellent team called International Summer Projects (ISP). ISP promoted ten different summer projects overseas. It was radical! Another national office promoted an additional 25 summer projects in the USA. There were offices both nationally and regionally that focused on these projects. The staff leading these teams and working in these offices were impassioned, called and committed. They produced excellent speakers, conferences, retreats, films, letters and brochures—all designed to get people to sign up for these projects and go to the ends of the earth.

But what did our KS-MO-NE campus ministries see from all of this vision and passion? How many of the 1,200 plus students went on these projects? Did vision (seeing the need) and passion (feeling the need) lead to mission (doing something about it)?

Well, no. Not really. We routinely saw about 200 go on U.S. Summer Projects annually. But only ten on average from 1980-1984 went on International Projects to the world.

This weighed heavily on me—very heavily. God allowed this burden to fan the flame of prayer for our staff, students, leadership and the world.

Nehemiah fed my soul. He carried a similar burden. Before being used to rebuild the wall in Jerusalem, God burdened Nehemiah with the sorrowful tragedy of it all. For months the burden weighed heavily on his heart until he took personal action and pursued the vision of rebuilding the wall, renewing the people and restoring God's glory.

God was sharing the burden of His own heart for the nations with all of us.

:: The Vision and the Worldwide Student Network ::

(Kansas City 1985)

"Although the Lord has given you bread of adversity and water of affliction, He, your Teacher will no longer hide Himself, but your eyes will behold your Teacher. Your ears will hear a word behind you, 'This is the way, walk in it,' whenever you turn to the right or to the left."
—Isaiah 30:20-21 (NIV and NASV)

"If at first, the idea is not absurd, then there is no hope for it."
—Albert Einstein

"There is one thing stronger than all the armies in the world, and that is an idea whose time has come."
—Victor Hugo

I had been an Area Director for almost seven months with this burden growing heavier each day, when one day in February 1985 I was visited by what I've often called a "vision." I realize that sounds a bit strange. Let me explain.

There was no audible voice. There were no pictures in my mind. No trumpets, angel's wings or halos. It was nothing spectacular, but it profoundly influenced me. My heart was captured. My mind was awake. Ideas flooded. I was carried along in what seemed like a dialogue between two hearts—God's and mine. I can only describe this "vision" as an impassioned conviction with specific words that became a striking calling of what I was to do.

Here's how it played out.

All of the staff from Kansas, Missouri and Nebraska met in the Doubletree Hotel in Overland Park, Kansas for a weekend retreat in February of 1985. I invited my old friend and long-distance mentor, David English, to be the Bible teacher and speaker for our retreat. David was always a treasured mentor in my life. He loved me so much and had so much wisdom, that I cherished every moment I could get with him. Getting with him wasn't easy though. David served as Regional Director for Eastern Europe and lived in Vienna, Austria from 1978-1984, while overseeing nine nations. He worked directly with one of my heroes, Bud Hinkson. Bud was the one who initially planted the desire to go to the Eastern Block at a conference I attended in Kansas City during my junior year at Oklahoma University—over eight years prior to this retreat. Bud and David both kept in touch with Karen and me over the years, and no doubt prayed for us on many occasions to one day join them. As we got to know them, they both encouraged us to come to Eastern Europe and work with them to reach those blinded by Communist Soviet Ideology.

Let's go back to the story of "the vision."

David English came to Kansas City to speak at our Area Campus Staff Retreat. Having him speak was totally in line with what I described before. The U.S. Campus Ministry was constantly talking about the world. We wanted someone from the mission field to speak to us from the Word of God, to build our Great Commission theology and challenge us to go to the world. We were eager to hear what God was doing behind the Iron Curtain and what the needs were, too.

On the first night after the meetings, I was telling David what I was learning and about our burdens regarding how very few were going to the ends of the earth. From the combination of his listening ear, wisdom and the questions he asked me, the Lord entrusted a concrete idea that was full of hope and conviction. I was telling David that the staff in our area had vision and passion for the world. Many students did, too. What was lacking was a profound sense of responsibility. Then it hit.

> *"David, we are not going to the world because we are responsible for nothing in the world. Could the U.S. Campus Ministry and the International Summer Projects Office give me—give us as an "Area" (meaning the "Kansas, Missouri and Nebraska Area Campus Ministry")—one nation in Eastern Europe that no one in the whole world of Campus Crusade could go to, unless they were from KS-MO-NE?"*

I was asking him if all U.S. national recruiting efforts could stop for one country. I was asking all responsibility be given to us as an "Area Campus Ministry" (KS-MO-NE) for one nation. With most leaders this idea would have been immediately disregarded. But not with David, he was living way out of the box already. His smile indicated he loved the idea. My stream of thought continued, *"I'd like to say to all our students and staff, 'Please consider all the overseas opportunities and pray about going to the world, but know this. No one will go to reach the people behind the Iron Curtain in country "X" unless they are from KS-MO-NE.'"*

Did you catch what was said? That is the "vision" that changed my life completely. It centers on the word responsibility. That conversation took place in February 1985. Within just a few days a partnership between KS-MO-NE and Hungary was forged and I received all approvals for moving forward with this paradigm shift.

The following is a letter I wrote to the staff in the fall of 1986 explaining the heart and soul of our new partnership with Hungary. By then, one year after we'd begun, we understood more of what God really wanted us to do in *"Denmark"* (a codename we used for Hungary while under communism). This letter helps describe the essence of the vision.

> *"Responsibility implies obligation. One definition of the word responsibility is 'a cause, person or thing for which one is responsible.' Responsibility contains an important word—response. A response is something done in answer to a need. Therefore, the responsible people in the world are the people who are burdened by certain needs. These needs play a large part in what they give themselves to. These needs call them into action based upon their personal burden. These needs motivate them to respond. Proverbs 29:18 says that 'without a vision the people are unrestrained.' In other words, they are free to live life apart from God's law and do what they wish; not being responsible or obliged to anything or anyone.*
>
> *But if people have vision, they are restrained by that vision. It locks them in. It gives drive and motivation to their lives. People of vision, then, are people who respond; people that take responsibilities seriously and carry them out with joy.*
>
> *Can a person, then, have a vision for the world without being burdened to the point of having their lives changed by that vision? Vision should move us on to responsibility. It seems we should not be talking about "vision for the world" without really taking steps toward reaching it.*
>
> *Some staff within our Area went to Central Europe in 1981. They came back with 'a vision' for that part of the world. Their lives were changed. They prayed differently, gave more and sought God for His plans to return or go to another Eastern European country on a full-time basis. They had a vision for that part of the world. They were burdened by the need to the point that their lives had to get involved in meeting that need. God led our Area to this kind of a response. I now*

believe it is impossible, and even un-biblical, to have a vision without responding to it in some significant way.

A concern arises when considering the vast numbers of volunteers in the Body of Christ. The manpower potential is staggering. The concern is that very few are responding to the need for global evangelization.

So what do we do? Do we tell them about the limited nature of short-term mission zeal? Do we blast them with a biblical challenge from our hearts expecting them to respond immediately? Should we all feel guilty that we are not going ourselves?

No. Jesus did not do it that way. He nurtured them first.

We cannot expect things to change, or people to change, unless we provide them with an education of the needs of the world and missions. The Partnership between KS-MO-NE and Denmark was raised up by God to do just that.

The Partnership allows us to gain a specific burden for the grandiose needs that accompany fulfilling the Great Commission. It has caused many to respond. It has helped us learn what it will take to really reach the world.

And what will it take? Thousands upon thousands of people responding with their lives! People with focused attention to specific needs God is burdening them to help meet. It was once said that 'the world will be reached for Christ by many tired people.' I agree. It will also take people that have a personal vision for a specific region or country in the world.

We, as an Area Campus Ministry in KS-MO-NE, are gaining a vision and burden for one country—to come alongside those already serving there to help reach it for Christ. And with that vision, God is giving us a plan to help reach that entire country."

That is the vision God gave.

On that wintery night in February 1985, passion was lit and was accompanied by a striking conviction. It changed our lives and called us to specific action.

We became responsible for a nation—Hungary!

:: The Responsibility ::

KS-MO-NE and Hungary

(1984 - 1989)

"Great are the works of the Lord; they are
pondered by all who delight in them."

—Psalm 111:2

I n March 1985, one month after the vision was given and all approvals were received, Karen and I went to our annual National Area Directors Conference in Southern California. Over 100 national, regional and area campus leaders gathered.

By then, ideas became concrete, vision raged, prayers for Hungary began and 25 staff expressed a strong desire to take part on the first summer project in Hungary. During that month, we did not realize what God was about to do— the fire in Kansas, Missouri and Nebraska was getting ready to explode all over the U.S. Campus Ministry.

The Area of Affairs Director for Eastern Europe and Russia was slated to speak at the conference—none other than Bud Hinkson. Before coming to the

USA to speak at this conference, Bud talked with David English. Bud was told of the "partnership vision." He loved this paradigm-breaking idea—giving people responsibility to exclusively partner with staff and campus ministries of other nations.

Because of Bud's integrity, enthusiasm and global stature within Campus Crusade for Christ, the partnership vision was getting ready to take a huge leap forward. During one of Bud's messages at the conference, he shared our vision and plans to partner with Hungary. My colleagues listened intently. The way they responded was a work of God. Ready for a challenge and already envisioned for the world, other Campus Crusade Area Directors immediately began to ask for the responsibility of a partnership with other Eastern European nations.

By the end of the week, over one-third of the U.S. campus ministries representing hundreds of staff and thousands of students, were mobilizing for nations like Romania, Bulgaria, Poland, Czechoslovakia, East Germany and Yugoslavia (particularly Macedonia, Bosnia, Croatia, and Serbia).

With the partnership between KS-MO-NE and Hungary as a seed, a seed sown by the grace of God on display through hundreds of praying people, the "Area Campus Partnership" vision was launched nationwide.

The partnership vision began to change everything in the U.S. Campus Ministry. The newly formed Worldwide Student Network (WSN), as the U.S. Campus Ministry's sending agency, began in the fall of 1984. The WSN Leadership Team immediately embraced the partnership vision and it became the fuel for spreading their passion to send more laborers to the world.

Three strategies were pursued by WSN. The entry strategy for a partnership was to send students and staff to partnering nations on European Resource Teams (ERT). ERT was our codename for International Summer Projects to Eastern Europe. We had to use a codename for security reasons for all recruiting and reporting of ministry activity while this part of the world was under communism. From the vision and experience captured on a summer project, we pursued the second strategy—sending qualified STINT teams (Short-Term International teams) to key campuses for one to two-year assignments in those partnering nations. And, finally, we sought to send IRs (International Representatives) long-term.

It is remarkable what God did during those years. One of the most memorable things was sending over 325 students and staff on summer mission projects to Eastern European nations in 1986. That summer was our first mission project to Hungary for the KS-MO-NE Area Campus Ministry. In the three years prior to the partnership vision, KS-MO-NE sent about fifteen students on International Summer Projects. But in 1986, even after the Chernobyl incident, 76 students and staff went to Hungary—all from just eight campuses.

I stressed earlier that waiting was hard—we were mysteriously directed to wait before moving there. We now knew why. Never in our wildest imagination could we have foreseen that waiting was part of God's plan for Eastern Europe (as well as building our personal character and ministry experience). The "Area Campus Partnerships" that were forming from 1985-1989 were mobilizing thousands to serve in Russia and Eastern Europe. This radically changed the U.S. Campus Ministry's sending strategy with an increased capacity to send. We saw thousands go on summer projects and hundreds go on STINT or as IRs to many of those nations.

But our focus was Hungary. In fact, it was much stronger than our focus. For the staff and students on the campuses of Kansas, Missouri and Nebraska, Hungary was our God-given responsibility. Of course, not all individuals in our area had a heart for Hungary. Before we began our partnership, some were already invested in places like Russia and Japan. We were eager to honor and respect their commitment to those places. Yet in the fall of 1985, to promote unity and momentum for our partnership, we encouraged everyone, in some way, to be a part of reaching Hungary by crossing what we affectionately call the "bridges of responsibility." The following five bridges of responsibility became our sending strategy. We encouraged every campus, and each staff and student to make simple plans to help fulfill our responsibility in Hungary around any or all of the bridges. Here they are:

:: **PRAYING** ::   *individual prayer as well as mobilizing concerts of prayer for Hungary.*

:: **GOING** ::   *mobilizing and training others to go to Hungary on short-term projects, STINT (one to two year short-term missions) or long-term.*

:: **SENDING** ::   *through discipleship ministries send others, even if God is not leading the "sender" to go personally.*

:: **GIVING** ::   *giving and raising finances to meet the various needs of the mission overseas, including people and projects.*

:: **CULTIVATING** :: *committing to develop the people and projects started by KS-MO-NE for the Hungarian partnership. When people go on short-term mission's projects, they tend to come back with a slide show and forget the developmental responsibility they have. We made various plans that kept us focused on developing what we started (e.g., hosting nationals on our campuses, raising money, investing in training Hungarian nationals, praying, corresponding with students, organizing ministry care packages, etc.).*

In any mission partnership, these five bridges of responsibility will help maintain a strategic focus in order to make a concentrated, developmental mission impact in another nation.

The Psalmist desired to *"give thanks to the Lord"* with all of his heart in the company of all of God's people. He said:

> *"Great are the works of the Lord. They are studied by all who delight in them. Splendid and majestic is His work ... He has made His wonders to be remembered." (Psalm 111:1-4)*

The Psalmist also wrote, *"Not to us! No! Not to us! But to Thy name give glory!"* That expresses what is in our hearts as we look back on these important years of ministry. In the spirit of Psalm 111 we'd like to take you on a brief walk through those years by taking a quick look at what God did through the Hungary-KS-MO-NE Partnership. Here are just a few highlights:

Regarding prayer: from February 1985 through 1991, except for the summer months during those seven years, we can document that one office team in Kansas City, as well as the staff and students from eight campuses in KS-MO-NE, set aside an hour a week to pray for the nation of Hungary. That is almost 250 weekly prayer meetings! Amazing! All focused on praying for Hungary – the people, the ministry and that God both would awaken His Church and send revival to this people group. I believe God is still reaping a harvest from the prayers sown back in those days.

Regarding mobilized manpower: from 1985-2000

:: over 500 students and staff went on fifteen different five-week summer projects in Hungary. These were used by God in very significant ways to help reach Hungary for the Lord Jesus. Many of the staff, families and church leaders in Hungary today were led to Christ either directly or from the chain of events begun by the partners who went during this time.

:: over 100 served on Campus Crusade's STINT program and opened campus ministries in Budapest, Szeged, Debrecen and Pécs, Hungary (see map of Hungary in the Appendix for detail).

:: 22 full-time Campus Crusade staff members from KS-MO-NE took long-term assignments in Hungary. Some served a minimum of four years. Others are still there—living and serving—over 24 years now.

Regarding other vital resources strategic to mission advance:

:: hundreds of thousands of dollars were raised.

:: books were translated.

:: leadership development opportunities were given to our Hungarian staff on three different continents.

:: counseling was given to hurting staff.

What is highlighted above would be fiction if it weren't for the grace of God working in and through broken and praying people who refused to live for anything but His glory. To God be the glory, great things He has done!

Let's fast forward from the starting point of the KS-MO-NE-Hungary Partnership in 1985.

By the spring of 1988 our partnership was well-grounded. WSN was off and running with a great leadership team embracing the partnership vision. The U.S. Campus Ministry was beginning to send to the world as never before.

Finally, Karen and I felt released to go. In April of 1988, along with Dr. Bill Bright's passionate encouragement for taking the Gospel to the ends of the earth, we knew God was calling us to leave America and move to Eastern Europe.

There was no turning back.

We moved to Hungary in 1989 just as the Iron Curtain was beginning to become a tattered veil blowing in the winds of change—winds of change caused by the love of God for the people of Eastern Europe and Russia. For decades under communism, God's love compelled His Church to press on. The Hungarian Church faithfully endured persecution for over 40 years, while the Body of Christ worldwide prayed for the suffering church and for the lost ones afflicted by atheistic ideology.

The waiting was over. The foundation was laid. Little did we realize what God was preparing to build.

Little did we know that my future best friend was also being prepared for a harvest both of us cherish to this day!

Section Five

:: **Behind the Iron Curtain** ::

:: Arrested and Free! ::

(Hungary 1967 - 1985)

Gábor's story from behind the Iron Curtain

"Enlarge the place of your tent, stretch your tent
curtains wide, do not hold back..."

—Isaiah 54:2

I t was a hot summer day in 1985. I enjoyed the cool water of Lake Balaton in Hungary. As I was walking out from the lake and went to my towel on the beach, two policemen came up to me. They were from a secret police unit in Hungary that is similar to that of the Russian KGB.

"You have to come with us!"

I was 18 years old. By this age, I had heard a lot of things about the methods of the Communist Secret Police. Our family suffered a lot under this regime. I had heard stories about how four of my relatives died in concentration camps. I knew that the Soviet Army had taken all of our family's wealth and had sent my great uncle to the Soviet Gulags for eleven years. During those years, his wife didn't hear anything from him. My Grandmother shared with me many times how their home and wealth were taken from them. She told me that they were deported to a little village that basically held them as prisoners. They could not leave that village, by law, for a decade. I had heard about the multitudes of people that simply "disappeared" in the dark cellars of the building known to be an interrogation center—the Communist House of Terror on Andrássy út 60 in Budapest.

Now they were here to take me.

I didn't know what to expect, although I knew why they had come after me. I had done something that was forbidden behind the Iron Curtain. Growing up in the communist regime, I knew very well what I was supposed to believe, think, feel, say and do. It was crammed down my throat for years. It was shouted in my ears. I was forcefully taught. Every child in Hungary learned very quickly the boundaries of belief within which they were to live. Brainwashing began at a very early age. The losses that our family experienced taught me early where I was supposed to mark my borders, but I couldn't help it. I had to cross the line. I knew I crossed it, too, but I thought I could get away with it.

I started crossing that invisible line in 1981. As I entered high school at age 14, I began denying being a member of the Young Communist Party (KISZ). My teachers were very upset with my decision, too. They would say, *"You are slitting your own throat, Gábor. This is stupid. No one can be an enemy to himself. What you are doing will only hurt you!"* They were warning me. If I did not join KISZ, I would have very little chance of attending a university or getting a good job in the future.

But I absolutely hated everything in this evil regime. I hated that we had to sing "hymns" to Lenin—Soviet Communist leader Vladimir Lenin. It was like worshiping him as we sang. It upset me to see Soviet soldiers on our Hungarian streets. I hated that they changed our street names. For example, our grand boulevard in Budapest known to Hungarians as the Elizabeth Boulevard was named after one of our most beloved queens. It was changed to "Lenin

Boulevard." Oktogon Square was changed to "November 7 Square" to celebrate the day the Bolsheviks seized power from the Czar in Russia (November 7, 1917). How audacious! Street names were changed in every major city in Hungary, and remained that way for forty years. Imagine your reaction if the Washington Monument was named after Ho Chi Minh or Osama Bin Laden. Their arrogance offended me deeply. They placed Soviet history and heroes all over our nation, while removing our very own. Statues of Lenin, Marx and Engels filled our capitol's streets. It filled me with anger that we had to stand in lines to get basic food. Our economy was weak. The lack of freedom to travel or to have free press irritated me. Only the privileged were given telephone lines.

Frustration grew to anger, and anger became hate. I wanted to express it, too. I wanted to do something to change our political situation. As early as my freshmen year in high school, I got involved in a political underground movement. My poor mother was very concerned. On top of raising my sister and me alone, she worried a lot about me. I was 15 years old, attending underground meetings and reading forbidden, secret material that came from the free world. I was not just reading it—I was making copies on my typewriter and passing out those copies with my friends. One of those friends in particular, was my girlfriend, Edina, who later became my wife. I knew Edina's grandfather's story. He was a Baptist pastor who suffered a lot under communism because of his faith. I had also heard how he was arrested because he gave Russian Bibles to Soviet soldiers. With a Masters degree in theology (ThM), he had to work as an unskilled worker in a factory to support his family. Meanwhile, the Church was compromising—submitting to every directive that came their way from the Communist Party. Edina's grandfather was not willing to compromise the truth of the Gospel, even if most around him were cowards.

I wanted to be a revolutionary. I could not accept the status quo. Edina shared my values and desires, too. Her radical nature was the first thing that attracted me to her. I was already a Christian at that time, but my focus was still on the Iron Curtain and seeing deep political change.

I grew up in a home that believed and followed the Communist Party line. My family denied the very existence of God. I didn't even hear the name of Jesus until I was 13 years old. Our family suffered many losses over two generations, as I mentioned before, including income, jobs, health and property. Without the faith to endure, those losses caused my father to become a very angry and abusive person.

His explosive anger led to my parent's eventual divorce when I was 8 years old. For some strange reason, the judge decided that my sister should live with my mother and that I should live with my father.

Living with him was sheer misery. He constantly threatened me. Eventually, I felt that my very life was at stake. I endured my father's anger for four years, but at the age of twelve, I ran away from him.

My father's abusive nature created very deep scars in my soul. It affected my personality. I had become a very fearful person. I was depressed. I suffered from severe asthma attacks. I was physically sick all the time. I was so sick that when I was 12, just four years after living alone with my dad, the doctors attending me predicted that I would not live past the age of 18. Imagine a 12-year-old boy, otherwise normal in every way, who had only a few more years to live. This caused me to withdraw from people. In fact, I didn't really want to be around anyone at all. I stuttered. I had a horrible inferiority complex. I had panic attacks. I was desperate each and every day. Every night I felt like dying. That's why I ran away.

Running away from my dad forced another court battle between my parents. After long deliberations, the judge decided that I needed to be protected from my father. I was granted the right to live with my sweet mother again. My dad did not even have the right to see me because of a restraining order issued by the court.

At that time of my life, God brought a young man into our family who talked about Jesus. I had never ever heard anything about God before. He was the first person I had ever met who believed in God. He told me that God could become my Father—that He is very loving and caring. He told me that Jesus died for me. I wanted to enter into a father-son relationship with Him through Jesus Christ. I decided to accept Jesus Christ as my Savior and Lord when I was 13 years old.

As I started this relationship with Him, God started an incredible healing process in my life. By His grace and power I was able to forgive my father. This forgiveness healed my wounds and brought real freedom into my life.

As God was leading in my spiritual journey with Him, I soon came to realize that there was a greater revolution to pursue than merely a political one.

Learning to forgive my father and being healed from my wounds was a long process for me. I was living behind a double Iron Curtain—one around my nation and the other around my heart.

The source of my deepest pain did not stem from the political system. The fear I experienced that summer in 1985 when the secret police arrested me was nothing in comparison to the fear I felt from my father while growing up. I was a slave to fear and paralyzed by it. The intimidating, angry words of my father, along with his unloving, selfish and abusive actions, imprisoned me more than anything else. I felt that everything I would ever become in life was being determined by the words my father spoke to me.

But my heavenly Father's Word started to have a greater impact on me. His loving, gentle and comforting words started to heal my soul. His words in Isaiah 54:2-3 became a personal life-changing promise that brought unknown freedom to my life:

> *"Enlarge the place of your tent, stretch your tent curtains wide, do not hold back; lengthen your cords, strengthen your stakes. For you will spread out to the right and to the left; your descendants will dispossess nations and settle in their desolate cities."*

Little did I understand in my teenage years how much the Lord wanted me to stretch and enlarge my borders! I was now starting to believe that the Lord could and would use me beyond the borders of my pain and experience. I began to believe that there is a life beyond my own spiritual Iron Curtain— beyond the limits that seemed to hold me back. There is a life "out there" with God, somewhere I had not yet walked. There is a place where fears, wounds and haunting memories would not be able to hold me back. Hope was trying to lighten my heart.

I had the first taste of hope in 1984 as God spoke to me through the Isaiah passage. I had arrived at a turning point on my spiritual journey. I took the first steps of crossing my own borders, as God exposed me to the following truths.

1. *I discovered that God can and wanted to use me for greater things than I could ever imagine.* God used a special person to make me understand this truth. Bud Hinkson was Campus Crusade for Christ's Area Director for Eastern Europe and Russia. I had never met a person like him before, or since, for that matter. I had never met anyone who was that close to Jesus. His passion, vision and love for the lost and for God changed my perspective about everything. I will never forget Bud sharing his vision to reach our closed country with the Gospel. He spoke with conviction and helped me see that God can and wants to use weak, poor and incapable people—just like myself.

2. *I experienced that evangelism works and is God's greatest work.* I learned to share my faith with people I had never met before. I went to an underground Christian training held by a small group in a tiny apartment in Budapest. Years later I learned this group was Campus Crusade for Christ. After the training, I went to a park and approached someone with a simple evangelistic booklet— one that I personally typed out on my typewriter. I was doing something that I had never dared to do; talking to someone about Jesus—something that was forbidden by our communist government.

I remember feeling something really great—that God can use me! After that experience, evangelism became my passion. I loved going to dorms and sharing Christ with students who had never heard anything about Him. I enjoyed the mixed feelings of evangelism. There was risk involved. We knew we were doing something that threatened communism. But the courage of my peers and the power of God in the Gospel made it thrilling.

3. *I understood the simple truth of walking by the power of the Holy Spirit.* The simple truth of "spiritual breathing": exhaling to confess my sins and inhaling by asking the Holy Spirit to fill, empower and control me. This kind of breathing changed my walk with God. Until this point in my life, I had tried to please God from my own strength and had failed.

Understanding and experiencing these truths radically influenced my life and changed my focus! I began to realize that there was a much more daunting kind of Iron Curtain than what I had previously been fighting against. The Iron Curtain I had been fighting was putting up external boundaries in people's lives: political dictators were limiting our freedom from the outside. But the more formidable Iron Curtain is internal. It is the Iron Curtain that surrounds our hearts, making us prisoners. It is our own sinful and unbelieving nature that creates a false sense of security and independence from God.

I realized that the real danger is living under the dictatorship of self. The real captivity is being imprisoned by our own sinful nature. I was beginning to understand that real freedom could never come from political change. God was beginning to focus my attention on another kind of revolution. A revolution of the human heart!

However, when the secret police came to the beach on that hot summer day, for a brief and fearful moment, all my courage to be a revolutionary went away with the warm summer breeze. I knew that they would try to stop me from sharing Christ. I knew they would not let me attend seminary (I wanted to be a Presbyterian Pastor because I saw that as the best option and only way to serve God full-time). I knew there could, in all likelihood, be other consequences as well.

During the interrogation at the police station in Siófok on that hot summer day in 1985, they attempted to stop us from sharing Christ with people. The police wanted to know everything—who we were, who we were with, why did we use the Four Spiritual Laws and more. They told us that we could not talk to anyone about Christ. By God's grace we told them that we could not stop. They searched my mother's apartment where I was staying and confiscated all Gospel literature we were using.

After the interrogation they released me, but did not allow me to attend seminary until one year later. I was forced to take the course by correspondence because they said, *"You have a bad influence on the communist development of our youth."*

God confirmed His promises in a supernatural way that summer.

A revolution had begun to unfold.

:: The Earthquake ::

(Siófok, Hungary August 15, 1985)

"After they prayed, the place where they were meeting was shaken."

—Acts 4:31

The summer of 1985 ended with something unforgettable. It seemed to foreshadow the fulfillment of the outrageous promise that would come almost a decade later. It was evidence of God's love and power. It forever confirmed to my soul that He listens to prayer.

There were about 15 young men and women involved in the ministry of Campus Crusade for Christ in Hungary at the time. All were passionate for God and actively trying to share His love with others. We were together in Siófok, at Lake Balaton, for a "Bible Camp" that lasted for two weeks. In the morning we would listen to lectures, study the Bible and discuss what we were learning. Each afternoon we would share our faith on the beach.

On the final night, we came together to pray for the entire night. We prayed for God to tear down the 'Spiritual Iron Curtain' around peoples' hearts.

We spent the whole night in prayer in my stepfather's tiny lake house near Lake Balaton in Siófok. I remember praying through Acts 4:23-31. We chose this passage because we had experienced a little persecution that summer from communist sympathizers and the police. It seemed appropriate for us to pray what the first century believers prayed when Peter and John were persecuted before the Sanhedrin. We didn't have their level of persecution, but being intimidated by the Communist Secret Police and answering their questions was scary enough for us.

Then it happened. We were praying through Acts 4:31. It reads:

> *"After they prayed, the place where they were meeting was shaken. And they were all filled with the Holy Spirit and spoke the word of God boldly."*

Immediately, around 5:00 a.m., just as we were praying this passage, the whole town of Siófok shook. It felt like a giant train ran just beneath our feet. It was loud, and everything was moving and shaking violently around us.

It was the largest earthquake in the history of Hungary, registering 5.2 on the Richter scale. The earthquake was felt in every shore town along the southern side of Lake Balaton. No one was hurt, but it caused great damage bringing unfortunate and costly loss.

To this day, everyone that was there still talks about that night. I imagine that none of us will ever forget it. It certainly marked my life. I don't think the timing of the earthquake was coincidental—hitting just as we finished praying through the Acts 4 passage. I believe that God wanted us to know He heard our prayers! He was confirming and communicating this to us in an unusual way, no doubt, but to come to any other conclusion seems irresponsible.

Keep in mind that we were minority Christians in a communist world and had just recently experienced persecution. This was an intimate way for God to promise us that He will answer prayer to open our country so that His Church could freely share the Gospel!

When the earthquake occurred, we could not have imagined what would happen next. We had absolutely no idea of the political and spiritual earthquakes that God was preparing to bring! God shook the Earth to let us know He heard our prayers just before He shook the gates of the Iron Curtain.

God was writing the prologue to a story that would change our lives forever. We were still four years away from what seemed like an eternal impossibility: the fall of the Iron Curtain. It had been standing strong for over 40 years all across Eastern Europe, with its Soviet mother reigning in the USSR for over 70 years. It seemed nothing would bring down communism or 'The Curtain.' We were still almost a decade away from God opening a wide door for the Gospel in the Hungarian educational system. Communists controlled everything in Hungary, but none more important than the door to every classroom in every school. Nothing could open doors to public schools. Or so it seemed.

But prayer would change everything we previously thought impossible.

Oddly enough, also in 1985, 7,000 miles away, university students and Campus Crusade staff in KS-MO-NE had been led to pray for a nation they had yet to visit. They prayed with passion previously unknown to them. At the time of the earthquake, all of us in Hungary did not know even one of them. Looking back on it now, I smile. God had mobilized His children, my future friends and partners in ministry, to pray for our nation. They were passionately living for Jesus in a different place, but joining us in prayer before the very throne of the Almighty God.

The "Partnership Vision" and the "Earthquake Experience" were signs of what God was ready to do—both touching the hearts of His children and confirming to them that prayer has power.

:: The Walls Have Fallen ::

(Eastern Europe 1989)

"This piece of barbed wire is a part of the 'Iron Curtain' alongside the Hungarian-Austrian border that demonstrably represented the division of the European continent into two halves. Its dismantling was made possible by the will of the Hungarian people and their recognition that peaceful co-existence and mutual interdependence is possible. We believe that the artificial, physical and spiritual walls still existing in the world some day shall collapse everywhere!"

—From an inscription on an official Hungarian plaque with a piece of the Iron Curtain attached. This plaque sits on Dave Robinson's office desk.

Another kind of earthquake had begun to unfold in the Hungarian society. This earthquake hit the very core of our political system. Limited free enterprise in business, granted in the early '80s, whet the appetite for more. The Hungarian people were growing tired of Soviet Communism. Many things led to the fall of the Iron Curtain, but none is more important, none more obvious to us as believers, than the fact that God had led His Church worldwide to pray.

The years just before the fall of communism were a time of preparation for us as a young campus ministry in Budapest. Evangelism and prayer became the two pillars of our ministry. We were just a small group of Hungarian students that began to associate with a small group of Americans and together we shared our faith with Hungarian university students. They were missionaries with Campus Crusade, unbeknownst to us at the time. We did not even know their real names. Every American, for security reasons, had a codename.

Security was a huge issue for ministries behind the Iron Curtain. My baptism characterizes the kind of security issues with which we had to deal. In 1987 an American pastor, Error! Contact not defined., came to our secretly held summer camp and baptized a few of us at Lake Balaton. He conducted it in the dark at 10:00 p.m.

In 1989 Edina and I were engaged to be married. We shared the same passion and calling to help fulfill the Great Commission. I knew she was a radical person. After all, we first met at underground Christian meetings. When I saw her passion for evangelism, my heart quickly fell in love with her. We started to share our faith in Christ together, pray together and dream together.

During those years the ministry started to grow. We went to more and more campuses as the grasp of communism became lighter and lighter each year. The pillars of this evil political system were shaking. The winds of change were blowing. Those winds brought unexpected and unimaginable change in 1989—change that would alter Hungary's history forever.

It was not, however, our first huge change. Our history is one of dynamic change and filled with unknown heroes. For example, in the middle Ages, the Hungarians turned back the Turks in their northern march to take over Europe, attempting to make it a Muslim continent. In 1956, it was the Hungarian students and factory workers who kicked the Soviets out of Budapest. The rest of the world watched passively as the Soviet Army reclaimed the city three days later, killing thousands and enslaving the Hungarian people with revived force.

But the change that came in 1989 was definitely new. Now we were at the threshold of freedom and democracy for the first time in our history.

In the spring months of 1989, the government announced there would be free elections one year later. Then, on May 2, 1989, Hungarian soldiers began dismantling the Iron Curtain along the Hungarian-Austrian border. (It was another six months before the Berlin wall fell.)

Long awaited freedom had arrived!

Millions of unknown heroes had been praying for over 70 years all around the world for something like this to happen. The evil regime of communism in Eastern Europe and in the Soviet Union had begun to collapse.

With God all things are possible. What seemed to be the impossible became a reality before our very eyes and it happened deeply, quickly and genuinely! God was truly changing history. History is truly His!

A passage of Scripture that is deeply loved by many of our colleagues regarding this miracle is Psalm 107:15, 16.

> *"Let them give thanks to the Lord for his unfailing love and his wonderful deeds for men, for he breaks down gates of bronze and cuts through bars of iron!"*

The Iron Curtain had fallen! The bars of iron of our prison's gate had been cut through. We were finally free! Millions of lives were sacrificed over the decades in Eastern Europe to have what we now have!

What a privilege! What a responsibility! Overwhelming joy and hope punctured the deep darkness of depression and suffering in our nation. The most significant event in Hungary's history happened in our lifetime. We were the first generation in the thousand-year-long history of our nation to experience democracy!

In all honesty, the excitement of this historic event was mixed with apprehension. Important questions had to be answered. Can a beaten down and tired people who suffered under communism handle the responsibilities of freedom? Could an entire society unlearn everything that was in its DNA for generations? Learning to live with freedom—a freedom that arrived so suddenly and changed everything—is not an easy process. The successful acclimation to freedom by the next generation was uncertain.

As believers, we knew that political change was not enough. A spiritual awakening was needed. The church in Hungary was still standing and many faithful leaders were ready to lead her forward.

We were eager to share the Gospel with our people, many of whom had never heard it even once.

God was preparing partners, too. From three small states in the middle of America, hundreds were being envisioned and prepared to come to our aid. Together, we would soon take strong advantage of our newfound freedom.

:: The Early Years in Hungary: Impossible ::

(Budapest 1989 - 1990)

The Robinsons move to Eastern Europe.

"He said this to test Philip."

—Jesus in John 6:6

From 1978 – 1989, back in the USA, we served in the U.S. Campus Ministry with Campus Crusade. We finished our training, enjoyed various ministry experiences and received invaluable input from great leaders. Karen and I had built a strong support team that was committed to pray for us and sacrificially give to our ministry. During those years, I had the privilege of attending Southwestern Baptist Theological Seminary and was ordained for the ministry by the Evangelical Church Alliance.

We had waited. God made sure of that. Altogether, it was 13 years of waiting—from 1976, when I was called as a university student, to 1989. We were more than ready to move to Eastern Europe. Our last year in the U.S. Campus Ministry was the school year of 1988-1989. God's faithfulness was clearly evident that year, as we made our transition to Hungary. He had raised our support, provided an excellent team of co-laborers and prepared us each step of the way.

It finally happened. In the summer of 1989, we moved to Budapest. Our oldest, Abbie, turned seven that summer. Dan was 4 years old. Our youngest, Katie, was just ten months old.

We were awakened from the more romantic aspects of our call rather quickly. The trials that hit us during the first seven months in Budapest were like none other in our lives before or since. Although Karen was shining bright in her faith, I was devastated. The cultural differences were huge. After a few months, I was at the rim of depression. I thought I had made the biggest mistake of my life.

The contrasts between Hungary and the USA were severe. Budapest was different from Kansas City in every possible way. Budapest looked different. Our eyes were assaulted by diversity. Signs were plastered on each pole and lined every billboard and building like wall paper. Every single word was unintelligible. The whole city seemed to be the color brown. Concrete was everywhere. The city was dirty. Poor, depressed faces surrounded us. We even noticed that street people regularly fed themselves from our trash cans.

Budapest sounded different. Buses roared. Trabants, the twin engine car built during the communist era, bleated. Dogs barked—all the time. Strangers greeted us with smiles, but in a language I could not understand. We couldn't help thinking that the tone of their voice indicated they might be angry with us.

Budapest smelled different. Smoke from burning leaves filled the air during the entire fall season. The relatively little air pollution for a city the size of Budapest still stifled us. We were used to pristine suburbs and the green, new beauty of Johnson County in the Kansas City area of Kansas.

These differences actually intrigued us at first, but that would change. It was language-learning that slowly chipped away at my confidence. During the seven months of intensive language acquisition, my enthusiasm for God's call and belief in His desire to use us in Hungary was severely threatened.

Learning the Hungarian language was our highest priority. I started classes in early September 1989, just five weeks after our arrival. On the first day of language learning my instructor made a statement that would soon rock my world. He declared that, next to Mandarin Chinese and Arabic, Hungarian is the third most difficult language in the world to learn.

By October, stress-filled homework had replaced my previously intimate quiet times with the Lord at 5:30 a.m. each and every day—five days a week. Up until that point, I was three years into a habit of spending up to an hour and a half with the Lord before starting my day. That was fading.

By Thanksgiving of that fall, I began to walk into a darkness of doubt that left my mind divided, my emotions dry, my heart cooling down and my will paralyzed. For a period of three weeks, due to the difficulty of learning the Hungarian language combined with a genuinely out-of-balance lifestyle, I began to wake up night after night in cold sweats trying to speak simple Hungarian phrases, but to no avail. *"Hang the picture on the wall"* was the phrase in many of my dreams that awakened me most frequently during that time. As I look back now, it seems ridiculous. But I could not control my tongue to say that insignificant sentence. I couldn't. It was impossible.

Once awake, after the sweat ventured down my back and the muffled Hungarian faded from my confused mind, a very clear voice was heard. Satan was there, as the accuser, trying to lead my mind astray.[1] The enemy of my soul immediately reminded me that I came to Hungary to say things much deeper and more meaningful than *"hang the picture on the wall."*

Well, of course, I did! This really bothered me. Karen and I had come to share the deep, deep love of God with the atheists of Eastern Europe. We came to joyfully persuade people with masterful apologetics who had never heard a clear presentation of the Gospel. But what difference could I make? I couldn't even say, *"Hang the picture on the wall."*

I felt like an idiot.

---

1. 2 Corinthians 11:3

Learning the language and making an impact for Christ seemed unthinkable. There were times that I would stand before our front door and stare— sometimes for minutes. I didn't want to go outside. As a sanguine, lover of people who finds renewed energy from being with others, I was lost in the discovery of this new dilemma of mine. I was reeling in wonder, seriously considering the possibility that I had missed God's call and muddled up the mission He had given me.

Maybe I was too eager, but my heart was good. Yet, I found myself in a stupor of regret and fear. I had a long way to go. It seemed dark and felt impossible.

IMPOSSIBLE screamed at me, *"Not capable of being done! Not capable of being endured!"* That is the nature and character of this word, impossible. It leaves us feeling ridiculous. It claims that what we face is going to crush us, the problem we deal with is without solution and what we seek is unattainable. Impossible! Every language has this word. It is *"lehetetlen"* in Hungarian. It is a word that stops us dead in our tracks. It immobilizes us! This is a word that straightjackets us as Christians and cries against our faith in God, *"ABSURD!"*

Close to it in the English language and very much related, is the word *"imposition."* To impose means that something makes a very strong impression of anxiety or produces a phenomenal emotional or physical burden because of its great size or strength. It is a Goliath that mocks and challenges us. It is a fiery furnace that brings great fear. It is a Red Sea that leaves us cornered with no way out! That is what I felt.

Our enemy is effective. He has so bound the army of God that we've been robbed of thinking we are strong enough, mature enough and secure enough to even make it through our personal struggles. But God wants to use us to radically change the world and tear down enemy strongholds. We must learn how to resist the lies of our enemy so that we can love people joyfully and sacrificially in order to help heal a broken world.

My resistance was down. With my failure in language and Satan's accusations, I found myself grieving, confused and full of doubt. I thought I would never make it.

Boy was I wrong! God graciously and faithfully held my hand, taught me His Word and put hope in my soul. He blessed me in many ways to keep my hope afloat and restore my energy.

He gave me Karen. She was a soldier, lover, teacher and friend. Without her maturity, I would never have made it. That word—"maturity"—may sound strange in this context, but there is no better word to describe her. She is solid. She is soft. She is wise. She is strong. She is kind. She knows God and walks in the power of the Spirit. She has an encouraging perspective from God's Word to share at any given moment.

More than anything else, God's Word kept me alive. During the months of difficulty God used John 6 in my life to build my faith and give me hope. He challenged my concept of *"impossible"* and showed me how to face my difficulties by using a conversation Jesus had with Philip.

> *"After these things Jesus went away to the other side of the Sea of Galilee and a great multitude was following Him ... Jesus went up on the mountain and there He sat down with His disciples ... lifting up His eyes and seeing that a large crowd was coming to Him, said to Philip, 'Where are we to buy bread, so that these may eat?' This He was saying to test him, for He Himself knew what He was intending to do. Philip answered Him, '200 denarii worth of bread is not sufficient for them, for everyone to receive a little.'"*
>
> —John 6:1-7

In this story Jesus raises the problem of food. He wanted to feed over 5,000 people. Where is a bread store in the vicinity big enough to have that much bread? Impossible? Well, yes. They didn't have Wal-Mart's Regional Warehouse in that part of Galilee.

Philip raises another problem—the problem of finances. Even if they had a bread store to go to in order to feed these people, they did not have eight months worth of wages to buy the bread. So, Philip retreated into the shadow of his limited perspective with a smile on his face. Hours later he offended Jesus by rallying the troops (the rest of the disciples) to tell Jesus that if he had any compassion He should send them all home now!

Jesus rebuked them, *"You give them something to eat!"*

By saying that to them, Jesus clearly shows us that He loves the impossible so much that He will actually initiate faith challenges—like He did with Philip—to help our faith in Him grow. He wants to expand our hearts, our influence and our capacity to be used by Him.

God used this passage to get me through the first years of difficulty. He told me to realize that He initiated the challenge I was facing to test my faith. Jesus initiates impossible circumstances to teach us more about Him. He wanted me to be surprised by His power and to know His intentions and desire to use me!

He wanted me to respond with faith. *"He said this to test Philip."*[2] Tests are not games, but part of God's gracious plan to strengthen our faith. I discovered in this time of battle that trials have the potential to arouse my flesh or approve my faith. Trials reveal one of two things in us; either the selfish willingness of our flesh to cave into temptation or the steadfastness of our faith to continue to trust in Jesus. It's true. In times of trial, we either fall to the pressure of temptation by making selfish decisions or trust the Lord in the pressure.

God was showing Karen and me that trials prove what is there, deep in our souls, to show what needs to improve to keep us approved. Trials build our faith and expose the flesh that hinders us. Their purpose is to get us to trust the Lord and distrust ourselves.

Jesus did not ask, *"Hey, Philip, what are some reasons we couldn't feed these people?"* It was as though He was instead saying, *"I don't want you to try and figure it out. I want your faith! Believe in me!"* But Philip totally missed it. Philip

---

2. John 6:6

was thinking only of a grocery store and money—resources he did not have nor could not imagine being provided.

During the initial months of cross-cultural shock and language-learning fears, God led me to pray over and read this passage again and again. As I did, I kept hearing God say very intimately, *"What should Philip have said to Me that day, Dave?"* This question intrigued and invited me to respond by faith. What should Philip have said? As I mulled it over, the Lord showed me how to answer it. In Luke 7:7 the Centurion who wanted his servant to be healed said to Jesus, *"Just say the word!"* Jesus responded in a profoundly surprising way. Jesus told everyone that this was an example of the greatest faith He had ever seen. Imagine that! The greatest teacher who ever lived said that the greatest example of faith He'd ever seen was not from a Jew, but from a Gentile soldier. Jesus was telling me that I should respond to my trials the way Philip could have.

Philip could have said *"just say the word"* on that day in the late afternoon with 5,000 hungry people around. Better yet, I could say that now!

And I did. I made it my prayer. *"Jesus, this is impossible—the third most difficult language in the world and I'm 32 years old, too old for language-learning. I'm a father and missionary with many responsibilities. It seems impossible, but I've seen You create an abundance out of absolutely nothing before. What do you have in mind, King? What do you have in mind Almighty One, Worker of the Impossible?"*

That lesson strengthened my faith and carried me through language-learning, team unity issues, teaching ministry philosophy, making ministry plans and pressing forward despite all obstacles.

And there were plenty more obstacles to overcome.

:: Campus: faithful, yet very little fruit ::

(1989 - 1993)

"Be of sober spirit, be on the alert. Your adversary, the devil,
prowls around like a roaring lion, seeking someone to devour...
resist him, firm in your faith..."
—1 Peter 5:8-9

After the cutting of the Iron Curtain and fall of the Wall, it seemed everyone was willing to talk about God. The lid of communism was off. The suppression of truth was gone. Everyone wanted to take advantage of the newfound freedom to talk about what was once forbidden. I can remember talking to student after student for hours over coffee. Everyone was interested.

The change was irreversible.

Hungarian soldiers dismantled the Iron Curtain in May 1989. Despite this, the East German government continued to grant summer visas to their citizens to visit Hungary. By August 1989 many East Germans tried, and with the Hungarian Border Police's permission, successfully got through the border to

Austria. After that, the hurricane of change swept through Eastern Europe and the very Soviet Union itself.

On December 25, 1989 at Edina and Gábor's engagement party, all were watching on live TV as the much hated communist dictator of Romania and his wife, Nicolae and Elena Ceauşescu, were both executed. By the time Gábor and Edina were married in 1991, the Soviet Army had left Hungary and the communist regime collapsed all over Eastern Europe. The once untamable Soviet Union was a closed chapter in the book of history.

The excitement of the change in the political system influenced all of us in profound ways. Mission agencies started to come. Campus Crusade finally could emerge from the shadows of an underground status and start functioning legally. New churches were being planted by most missionaries, including many Crusade staff.

At the same time the vacuum in the society, created by being isolated from freedom for so many decades, sucked everything into the country that the Free World wanted to offer: the good and the bad. Almost everything was welcomed in a society that had been left incapacitated from its lack of values and morals for decades. Hungary was on shaky ground. It wasn't sure of its own standards. The insecure, demoralized and unstable society was not able to know the difference, in many cases, between right and wrong. Hungary's centuries old Judeo-Christian foundations were almost gone. So, when the post-modern messages of the Free World arrived in Hungary, it started to dominate the entire culture quickly. Suddenly, the Hungarian people faced issues they had never encountered on a large scale: sexual promiscuity, AIDS, drugs, gangs, new crime, cults and many economical and sociological challenges.

All of us knew this unprecedented moment in history demanded unique commitment.

Gábor and Edina wanted to take advantage of the new opportunities afforded by the change. Immediately after their wedding they got involved in church planting and helped start a new church in the 22nd district of Budapest. They felt called to be in full-time Christian ministry where they could focus on evangelism and discipleship. God led them to join staff with the group they had been serving in for eight years under communism. In 1992, they joined the staff of Timóteus Társaság (Campus Crusade of Christ, Hungary).

At that time, I thought that almost every conversation I had with people would lead to each person repenting of sin and placing their faith in Christ. Everyone seemed fascinated to meet a true believer in God and talk about spiritual things. Their questions were sincere. Their surprise at God's Word was staggering. Their hearts opened up, revealing deep needs that only Jesus could heal.

I remember Gergely, a 23-year-old, fifth-year student at the prestigious ELTE University in Budapest. We hosted a three-night lecture series called "The Philosophical Implications of a Universe Without God." Over 400 university students and professors attended this outreach. Gergely, wanted to meet with me to talk more about God after the series of presentations concluded.

The next day we sat down for coffee at a local café on the Pest side of Budapest. He identified himself as an atheist with no purpose in life. He believed that the only meaning in life is the meaning you create for yourself by the choices you make. Gergely found his personal meaning in sex and health. He was committed to being in great shape and worked at it diligently.

He admitted that sex and physical fitness were not enough to give him joy and significance. Yet, he was convinced that this was the only thing that made any sense. This was his life and the way he wanted to live.

His looks betrayed this, but as we spoke it became increasingly clear that he had a very dark side. He was depressed and had no shame in declaring it. He was sincere. In fact, he knew that as soon as he reached the point of not being in good shape, he would kill himself with pills, a razor blade and a warm bath. He was even preparing for that day.

Right at the beginning of our conversation, I noticed a deep wound on the back of his left hand. I said nothing about it, but as we continued to talk he explained why the wound was there.

Gergely said, *"I've been preparing for the pain of death at my own hand."* I asked him what he meant.

"You see this wound?" He then showed me both sides of his left hand. There was an ugly wound on the palm side, too. It looked like an inversed, worn, eroded volcano. He continued. *"It took me over two weeks to finally endure the pain of piercing my hand with an ice-pick, but I did it. This scar is two months old."*

He had it all planned out. Gergely would commit suicide on the day he no longer could do something physically—something very specific. Every day after class, he would walk home and go to the elevator in his building where he lived. The elevator doors would open, but Gergely would not get in. He would press the #4 button, the floor he lived on. Then immediately he would take off running. He'd race up the stairs in his building as quickly as he could.

Gergely was telling me this over coffee. He had a depressed, intelligent and nice looking young woman at his side. He finished telling me his story this way, *"The day the elevator beats me to the fourth floor is the day I die at my own hand."*

As I assured Gergely of God's love for him, I tried to persuade him that there was more to live for. *"God's love for you, Gergely, means that every moment of your life is valuable."* But nothing I said seemed to impact his thinking.

My encounter with Gergely was further evidence of the spiritual warfare that raged all about us. We had to learn to fight differently.

All of the Crusade staff would share their faith many times a week. We met all kinds of people. Again, all of them wanted to talk. Yet, precious few ever made a commitment to Christ and followed Him in faith.

Over the first 24 months of ministry, the team grew increasingly discouraged. God was breaking us to prepare us for a harvest of unthinkable dreams and unspeakable joy. Even so, more brokenness was coming as we launched into new territory.

:: Clumsy Attempts ::

(1992 - 1993)

"Brothers, think of what you were when you were called. Not many of you were wise by human standards; not many were influential; not many were of noble birth. But God chose the foolish things of the world to shame the wise; God chose the weak things of the world to shame the strong. He chose the lowly things of this world and the despised things — and the things that are not — to nullify the things that are, so that no one may boast before him."

—1 Corinthians 1:26-29

D ave had been the National Director of Timóteus Társaság (CCC, Hungary) for three years when we (Gábor and Edina) joined staff in 1992. With a great leadership team in place, all of us in Timóteus Társaság were seeking to step out into new territory and utilize the God-given moments of openness.

By the spring of 1992 we were beginning to grow in the campus ministry. God was giving His grace to broken people who united together in prayer. We had exciting outreaches with 400 to 1,300 students in the audiences. One outreach was very special. We hosted Dan Korem, a professional magician and investigative journalist who exposed spiritual hoaxes. He packed out our venue three nights in a row. Outside of our outreach events, many students were joining discipleship groups and about 100 students gathered each week at Műszáki Egyetem (The Technical University of Budapest) for our weekly meeting.

The Campus Ministry in Budapest had great leadership. Terry McKinney was National Campus Director at the time. Bruce Elliott was our National Training Director. Both of these Americans served to shepherd, model and support a growing campus ministry. Future leaders were being trained and beginning to take the lead. Hungarians on the Budapest local team were committed, qualified and envisioned for evangelism and discipleship. On that team were Varga Gyuri and Anikó, Kazár András and Sara, Ujj Andrea, Rácz Laci and Bea, Janurik András and Erika and Tárkányi Jutka.

Of course, we had a great partnership for campus ministry development with KS-MO-NE, too. We expanded the campus ministry in 1993. Trained men and women from our Budapest campus ministry allowed us to plant a new ministry in Szeged, a city in south-central Hungary just north of the Serbian border. The leader of that team was Rob Futó.

The campus ministry was on the verge of bearing lots of fruit. Leadership was in place. Disciples were being built up. The team was mature and united. The time had come to take a huge step of faith and launch beyond the campus into the community.

Dave and the National Leadership Team had cast a vision and now, in the summer of 1992, it seemed that Timóteus Társaság was ready to go. Paul and Lori Dickason were veteran missionaries in Hungary and strategic to the campus ministry in Budapest. However, seeing the need to expand our ministry beyond campus, Paul volunteered to pioneer and form a community ministry team. Dave appointed Paul the Community Ministry Director that summer. Edina and I were excited and anxious to get involved. We joined the newly launched

Community Ministry Team in the summer of 1992. Our team included a female athlete named Emhő Réka, Edina and myself.

Everyone on the team had a heart to pioneer. Yet, our experience was limited to campus ministry and university students. None of us knew how to reach out effectively into the community. We only knew that we needed to get to the *"influencers"* in the community, the change agents.

We tried hard. We tried everything. We made fools of ourselves. We were passionate. But as amateurs in this new territory of ministry, we didn't know where to start or how to get there. We only knew that we wanted to get the Gospel to people in the community.

As I look back on it, even our best ideas are a bit embarrassing to me now. No. It was embarrassing to me then, too. Go easy on me, reader. I'm going to tell you a couple of stories. You are going to smile.

One of our brilliant and creative ideas was to stand in front of grocery stores with the JESUS Film displayed on tables—little, ugly ones. We tried to convince people to sign up to borrow the film for free. As Dave always says when surprised by a bad idea, *"Whoa!"* It was a brave, bold and bad idea—not very creative at all. We had to do something, so we did. We did that! We were brave perhaps, but not at all very smart.

One week I carried my little table and stood in front of a grocery store, trying to get people to sign up and borrow the JESUS Film. The plan was that after viewing the film, we would go visit those who watched the film and talk about it. Each day I approached at least 100 people, but only 2-3 signed up. Some of them were in need of serious psychiatric counseling. I'm not kidding at all!

After visiting a couple of them and trying to talk to them about Jesus, and listening to their horror stories about their unfortunate lives, I realized that I was not suited to be a counselor and that this type of evangelism was not something I wanted to do for even one more hour.

This strategy was not leading us where we wanted or where we were called to go. Our calling was to reach the influencers in the community.

Are you smiling? We are not quite finished.

Some members on our team had even more bizarre ideas. One staff in the fall of 1993 joined a flower-cutting class so as to meet others and build friendships with non-Christians. Brave? Well, yeah. But, well, *"Whoa!"*

God still blessed us though, even while we were making these clumsy attempts. As we look back on it, we think our willingness to try anything for the glory of God and good of man attracted God's attention. After all, the Bible says He *"gives grace to the humble."* We excelled in humility. Imagine what we looked like in front of those grocery stores. I'm kidding a bit, but honestly, we just wanted to find a way to reach people effectively.

I said before that God blessed. How did God bless our clumsy attempts?

One time Edina and I volunteered to teach the Bible to first graders in a public elementary school in Budapest. Anyone who knows Campus Crusade will quickly note that grade school children are not our typical ministry target. Our thought in speaking to the children was that through them we could possibly reach their parents. We thought, *"Maybe this is how we can begin to reach influencers."*

You may be saying, *"Oh, my. This isn't very smart either."* You are right. But then again, we are not very smart people. The only virtue we may have had on display was passion.

We taught weekly in this school for the entire 1992-1993 school year. Going to that first grade class taught me another truth about myself: I'm not suited to be a teacher either.

YET…

…in the class where Edina and I taught was a 6-year-old little girl named Nóri. She listened well. She was a precious little pearl. Unknown to us at the time, God touched her heart and she became a Christian. We did not find this out until much later. Now 16 years later, she is a university student and one of the key student leaders in our ministry. Her younger sister Sári also came to the Lord and is now involved in our high school ministry in Budapest.

God will use anyone available to Him who is willing to do anything for His glory. We did not see this truth clearly then, but we certainly do now.

Nóri and Sári were unknown blessings at the time. What we felt was entirely different. We felt tired. We were discouraged. All of our attempts to reach the community were embarrassing flops. After months of working hard and trying so many different things, we did not see any fruit. As the student ministry was flourishing on campus, our little team was dying in the community.

Edina and I wanted to leave staff, leave the ministry and give up. I was not prepared for such a difficult harvest. The hardships of missionary life came with lots of unwanted surprises. My willingness to give up so fast is just more evidence of my own weaknesses. Outside of marriage, there was not one area of life in which I felt like a success. I was miserable. I was disappointed in the results. I was disappointed with Campus Crusade. But most of all, I was disappointed with myself. After all my zeal and sacrifice for many years under communism, I expected different results. I expected God to bless my efforts for Him, but He didn't. At least not the way I thought He would.

After just a few months on staff, in the spring of 1993, I applied for other jobs without telling anyone. I wanted out. After a short time I found a good job in a growing software company. I was glad—very glad. It felt like a miracle. After discovering all the things that I'm not good at and did not want to do in ministry—after all the embarrassing disappointments—things were turning around.

Around that time, I remember Dave sitting down with us in our cold, one-room, dark, moldy apartment. I told him that we were discouraged, ready to give up and were leaving staff. We talked and talked. God used that conversation to encourage us to go forward in the ministry. Dave reminded us of our vision, the times we were living in and of the hope that Jesus gives us as we follow

Him. I looked back and remembered the earthquake, the promises God gave to us and His personal calling. I had to learn that it is not my zeal, passion, enthusiasm or hard work that brings fruit in the ministry, but only Him. We began to think, *"Are we serving Him for the results (what He gives us for our hard work) or are we serving Him to glorify Him, no matter what the results were? What if we don't like how He wants to glorify Himself through our service to Him?"*

Finally, both Edina and I were ready and willing to do anything, anywhere, anyhow with anyone – whatever He wants us to do – regardless of the results.

Broken, yet yielding to Him, we pressed on. Nothing was working that well, but we continued to place our hope in the Lord. The breakthrough we were hoping and praying for was close, but came in an unexpected way.

Section Six

:: Youth at the Threshold of Life ::

:: Mark 9 and the Call to Prayer ::

(1991)

"This kind cannot come out by anything but prayer."

—Jesus

After the revolution in 1989, virtually every conversation we had with people about Christ was positive. Everyone we met was brought up in a communist system that taught Marxist-atheism. When Hungarian university students met someone who appeared intelligent and actually believed in God, their intrigue led to long and spirited conversations. We met with hundreds in coffeehouses all over Budapest and in various dorm rooms strewn across the city. No one was disinterested. Practically every conversation was about Jesus, the validity of the Bible, the existence of God or the history of Christianity. Every conversation was long, serious and riveting. It was a joy.

But very few placed their trust in Christ.

Over time it became very discouraging to all of us. Imagine having conversation after conversation when people asked great questions, heard profound historical and philosophical apologetics, engaged in discussion for hours and hours, month after month. Imagine how exciting that would be! It was. Yet we saw very few people actually become Christians. It became increasingly frustrating.

We did not know what to do.

In mid-February 1991, I met with Dan Butts, a missionary colleague with Campus Crusade. We talked and prayed about the meaning of this dilemma. Eventually, we looked at a text in Scripture that God used to re-direct our entire ministry.

Mark 9:14-30 changed our ministry forever. Read this slowly.

When they came back to the disciples, they saw a large crowd around them, and some scribes arguing with them. Immediately, when the entire crowd saw Him, they were amazed and began running up to greet Him. And He asked them, *"What are you discussing with them?"* And one of the crowd answered Him, *"Teacher, I brought You my son, possessed with a spirit which makes him mute; and whenever it seizes him, it slams him to the ground and he foams at the mouth, and grinds his teeth and stiffens out. I told your disciples to cast it out, and they could not do it."* And He answered them and said, *"O unbelieving generation, how long shall I be with you? How long shall I put up with you? Bring him to Me!"* They brought the boy to Him. When he saw Him, immediately the spirit threw him into a convulsion, and falling to the ground, he began rolling around and foaming at the mouth. And He asked his father, *"How long has this been happening to him?"* And he said, *"From childhood it has often thrown him both into the fire and into the water to destroy him. But if You can do anything, take pity on us and help us!"* And Jesus said to him, *"'If You can?' All things are possible to him who believes."* Immediately the boy's father cried out and said, *"I do believe; help my unbelief."* When Jesus saw that a crowd was rapidly gathering, He rebuked the unclean spirit, saying to it, *"You deaf and mute spirit, I command you, come out of him and do not enter him again."* After crying out and throwing him into terrible convulsions, it came out; and the boy became so much like a corpse that most of them said, *"He is dead!"* But Jesus took him by the hand and raised him; and he got up. When He came into the house, His disciples began questioning Him privately, *"Why could we not drive it out?"* And He said to them, *"This kind cannot come out by anything but prayer."*

This passage has so many similarities to what we were feeling and experiencing. God's voice was lighting our path and making our footsteps sure once again. For example:

:: Like the nine disciples, we were frustrated. Jesus' disciples had cast demons out of people before this event, yet for some reason lacked what it took to win this new battle. We lacked so much as well.

:: Like the demonized one, the enemy was free to rape Hungary with lies and sin for years and years—centuries in fact. Since her "childhood," Hungary had suffered as a nation from the hand of Satan—from the Muslim Turks, the Fascist Germans and the Atheistic-Communist Soviets.

:: Like the father of the demonized boy, our staff and student leaders were fearlessly and faithfully loving others and trying to help them gain the freedom that only Jesus and His Gospel can give.

:: And like them, we faced a battle that needed a new tactic.

But one thing was rudely missing from our battle plan: prayer. Earnest prayer needed to be infused into our tactics. Jesus taught His disciples that there is a type of spiritual battle that can only be won through prayer.

Over the course of a few days, the Lord led us to a firm decision. As the burden of not seeing much happen in ministry grew, and with this passage of Scripture emboldening me, I decided to ask the staff to call off ministry for three days each week in the month of March—no Bible studies, no witnessing—nothing. That was a bit radical for us. I was asking them to take off one month from normal ministry—the very best month of ministry for a campus worker. Normally, after reconnecting with students after their winter break from exams, we used February and March to do lots of outreach, hold a retreat and form discipleship groups. Giving up March meant a paradigm shift, a lot of adjustments in our schedule and changing our expectations, too. But the staff and students were eager to comply.

We prayed for a month! It was March 1991.

That month became a watershed moment in our lives. Not only did we pray and learn a ton about prayer, we confessed sin, sought the Lord in open worship and earnestly begged God for spiritual awakening in Hungary.

After this one month of prayer, three significant things happened. One, our staff seemed lighter in spirit and refreshed as they continued to work hard in ministry. Two, we saw more and more place their faith in Christ—over 200% more fruit came from our efforts in evangelism. As I share the third thing, I don't want to be misunderstood. This was a huge blessing, but I am not comparing this to the first two things that happened as a result of our prayer month—the staff having renewed energy for ministry and more coming to know Jesus. But the third blessing was just that, a blessing—a huge blessing.

We were growing as a ministry. More and more people were applying for staff. The JESUS Film ministry presented great opportunities for mobilizing local churches. We were translating and publishing more and more books for the Hungarian Christian community. Our office needs grew. Our first office was in a scrawny, old, dirty two bedroom apartment off of Kis János Altábornagy in Buda. Then we rented a second apartment on Stromfeld Aurél two blocks away. It was pretty inconvenient.

After the month of prayer we had a special visitor from the USA. A visiting supporter of one of our staff, a person who was an office manager by profession, saw our situation and was grieved. She was so grieved she went back and raised $100,000 for us to buy an office. This was the third blessing that resulted from our month of prayer. We had never seen this kind of money before. God was preparing us in 1991 for a future of miracles in many fruitful harvests that required millions and millions of dollars over the next 20 years. This was our first $100,000.

In the subsequent years, from March of 1991 forward, we canonized our prayer emphasis. We had months of prayer. We had weeks of prayer. We had prayer chains. We had prayer nights. We shared answers to prayer with regularity. We mobilized the church at *"Prayer and Fasting Retreats."* We dedicated two days every May (which still continues to this day) for remembering the great works of God in prayer.

We had another month-long prayer emphasis just before Christmas of 1993. We had expanded our campus ministry. That was going well. Yet, we were 18 months into the difficult fields of community ministry. As we gathered for prayer, we did not know it at the time, but God was preparing us for an *"Acts 2:47 Moment"* in the community ministry. Acts 2:47 reveals that the early Church experienced great fruit in evangelism. Day by day *"the Lord was adding to their numbers."*

That was getting ready to happen to us. The whole world had been praying for over 70 years for this part of the world. The entire Church of Hungary was praying with great zeal, too. A great harvest in Hungary had been sown— sown by tears, sown by faith, sown by prayer. A harvest shared by His Body nationwide was about to be reaped.

:: The Letter ::

(January 1994)

"The kingdom of heaven is just like a mustard seed."

—Matthew 13:31

As Paul says, *"Walk by faith, not by sight."* God can bring abundance out of absolutely nothing!

Prayer had become an important part of our ministry. The many barriers and unsuccessful attempts in ministry were used by God to get our attention. Since March 1991 we had made great strides forward on our knees. Yet, as blessed as we were, we were not prepared for the blessing that would follow our next prayer month.

In December of 1993, every staff serving with Campus Crusade in Hungary gathered for another "Month of Prayer." Every day we came together to worship and pray all day long. We were confessing our sins and also our nation's sins. We were praising God for His salvation. We were praying for awakening, for a breakthrough in ministry—something only God could do. We knew well where our efforts could take us—not far at all. Our ideas and zeal had serious limits.

We were asking God to break through – to cut through the bars of iron again. If He did it once, He certainly could do it again!

During this month of prayer, my (Gábor's) mother Mária began a new job at the National Institute of Health. She knew that, as missionaries, we had to raise our own support to provide the financial support for our ministry. Raising our own funds was, and remains, an incredible challenge for us in Hungary. There are very few churches with very few Christians in those churches with the monetary means to support such missionaries.

Edina and I not only needed money to live, but I badly needed a computer for our ministry, too. It was impossible to imagine that I would ever have enough money to buy a computer. My mother mentioned that we could write a fundraising proposal to the National Institute of Health asking them if they would be willing to donate a computer to us. She knew they had grant money to support groups who were working with young people.

I really needed a computer, so I convinced myself to try and write a fundraising proposal to the National Institute of Health (NEVI)[1]. In my proposal letter to NEVI, I mentioned how much I appreciated their efforts to protect young people from the dangerous and risky behaviors of drug-abuse, promiscuity and gang membership (the Skinheads immediately gained popularity following the fall of the wall).

In the letter, I also shared my conviction that the best way to prevent young people from these kinds of behaviors is to encourage them to know Jesus Christ personally. I closed my letter by informing them of what we did on staff with Campus Crusade (Timóteus Társaság). I mentioned that we help young people grow morally, intellectually, socially and spiritually. Then, I simply asked them to consider supporting our efforts by donating a computer.

As we look back on this letter now, we think of how God's sovereignty was at work. This was a fairly bold idea – telling a post-communist government

---

1. Nemzeti Egészségvédelmi Intézet in the Hungarian Language (NEVI)

agency that the best way to save young people is to share the Gospel with them, and then, encourage them to donate to that purpose! We weren't smart at all. Yet, God led us to send that letter anyway. It was in early January 1994, just a few days after the December Month of Prayer event.

A few days after we mailed the letter to NEVI our phone rang, but we did not hear it. My wife and I were in the kitchen, too far away for us to hear the phone. The person on the other end of the line did not give up. He continued trying to reach us.

Finally, we heard and picked up the phone.

"Hello! I'm Gábor. With whom am I speaking?" I asked.

The other person said, *"I am Dr. Dénes Bánhegyi. I am the National AIDS Coordinator for the Hungarian government. I have just finished reading your proposal – the letter you wrote came to me. I'd like to meet with you and talk. I'd like your director to come, too. Could we meet in my office in the AIDS hospital next week?"*

After arranging the time and the place of the meeting, I hung up the phone. I was standing there dumbfounded and motionless. This was an unusual phone call. I could not believe what I had just heard. He called me on the very day he received my proposal. He sounded urgent. I thought, "Why does he want to meet with me? Just give me that computer and we are done. Why does he want my director to come?"

None of us were ready for what was coming. A simple letter became the tipping point.

:: A Meeting in the AIDS Hospital ::

(St. László Hospital, Budapest January 1994)

"I know your deeds. See, I have placed before you an open door that no one can shut. I know that you have little strength, yet you have kept my word and have not denied my name."

—Revelation 3:8-9

B y January of 1994, our Community Ministry Team was only 18 months old. That team did the wildest things to try to break through to the community in Budapest. They were charged with pressing the battle lines further into society—pioneers from the campus to take our ministry beyond the campuses of Budapest. Carving a path for future ministry took bizarre turns. They joined swim clubs and flower cutting clubs. They sold books. They showed the JESUS Film. All attempts were pretty much without any lasting fruit.

One and a half years of faithful but fruitless pioneering had passed. Everyone on their small team grew tired and discouraged. It was understandable.

Paul Dickason, the team director, called me (Dave) one day in January of 1994. One of Gábor's support contacts wanted to meet with me. They had already arranged the meeting.

At that time, I did not know Gábor very well at all. Gábor and Edina Grész were two of the "faithful five" on the Community Ministry Team. Gábor was one of the original few that helped us launch the campus ministry as a student in the 80s. For years, he was a volunteer before joining our staff in 1992. We had known each other since 1985, but only casually. We'd never spent much time together. Our paths seldom crossed. He worked in an office I rarely visited. I was going on campuses and meeting with staff in their homes, hotel lobbies and coffeehouses all over Budapest. Gábor was working in one church-plant in Budafok. I was working in another church-plant in Budapest.

We were going to meet Dr. Dénes Bánhegyi, along with some of his colleagues, in the St. László Hospital where he worked as Chief of Immunology. Dr. Bánhegyi was also the National AIDS Coordinator appointed by the Hungarian government. He and his team were responsible for providing quality sex education to stem the tide of AIDS that many feared would sweep across Eastern Europe. They had millions of Forint[2] at their disposal. We didn't know any of this prior to that first meeting, but as we were looking for a breakthrough in the community ministry, we were eager to find out what God was up to.

I remember walking into the hospital for the first time. We were headed to the Immunology Department where the sickest people in Hungary wind up; people who are terminally ill, people dying of AIDS. At the time I knew very little about the disease. As Gábor, Paul and I walked in, we whispered to each other not to touch anything. We knew we could not get AIDS that way, but it made strong sense to us to keep our hands in our pockets.

We entered Dr. Bánhegyi's office and met with his leadership team from NEVI. Along with Dr. Bánhegyi, three delegates from NEVI and its National AIDS Committee met with Paul, Gábor and me.

Dr. Bánhegyi began by stating rather bluntly that he was looking for a new partner to help him carry the burden of sex education in Hungary. His

---

2. Hungarian monetary currency is called 'Forint.'

team had a huge social mandate and an even bigger political responsibility. They had been entrusted with preventing the worldwide AIDS epidemic from encroaching upon Hungary.

Prior to the fall of the wall, migrating across communist Eastern Europe was very difficult. To receive a tourist or travel visa you had to go through an intimidating process that included long lines, multiple offices and the growl of machine-gun-carrying police. After the fall of the wall, there was new freedom to travel within the former Eastern Block nations. In 1993 over 16 million visitors crossed the Hungarian border. They had never before seen numbers of people like this enter their nation in such a short period of time. People from all over the world came to visit, find a job or simply travel through Hungary in route to another destination. This new migration brought grave concerns to Hungarian health, civil and political officials. From 1990 (just a year after the revolution) to 1993 many destructive industries were growing and beginning to destroy the fabric of Hungarian society. The sex, prostitution, crime and drug industries were showing signs for exponential growth.

Sexually transmitted diseases and teen-age pregnancies were on the rise. Young people in their mid-twenties were contracting AIDS. These were Dr. Bánhegyi's greatest concerns.

His group was well financed, connected and had all the influence they needed to address these issues, but everything they tried had failed. Translating liberal sex education material from America failed with Hungarian parents and teachers. Attempts at finding partners had failed as well. A prominent church denomination even dismissed an invitation to help NEVI. So, they were looking for a new partner.

"Will you join us by writing a curriculum for our public schools?" Dr. Dénes Bánhegyi was serious. I was surprised at his request, but tried to hide it.

After asking questions regarding the need, the budget, and the behavioral targets we should aim for, I was eager to let him know we would do everything we could to help.

But I had to be brutally honest.

I mentioned that he came to the right people. *"We are part of an organization that has 100,000 university students involved and a network of approximately 10,000 university professors known as Campus Crusade for Christ and Christian Leadership (our ministry to university professors). In Hungary our organization is named Timóteus Társaság."*

I continued.

"Yet, on our staff team in Hungary we have no doctorates in education." I quickly added, *"We are, however, experts in these problems among youth."*

I was expecting a long silence, and maybe a few rolled eyeballs to bounce around the circle, but Dr. Bánhegyi shot back. *"Good. I've been working with our Hungarian educators for years now and they have no idea how to reach the young people of today. I want to know what you can do and I hope you can help me."*

We talked for about one hour. The Lord was so gracious to us during that brief time. He allowed us to ask the right questions, collect vital information, and honestly share our concerns and opinions.

All the while, God allowed us to remain poised. That was a small miracle. As I look back on it, I think I acted like things like this happen to us all the time. But if my spirit were to physically represent me during that hour, I would have been caught with my mouth wide open. I knew this was huge. But God allowed us all to remain calm and "professional." Something we had little experience in.

The most important information we discovered that day was the committee's heart for children. They wanted to revolutionize the Hungarian classroom for their sake. They wanted to help them learn values and life skills. Besides being obviously brilliant people and good leaders, the committee from NEVI showed real, down to earth savvy that morning, too. They knew that teachers, educators and parents needed to learn new ways to reach their youth effectively. This generation of youth was the first to be free from the tyranny of communism. Dr. Bánhegyi's team clearly desired the students of Hungary to get the attention and education they needed. They also had the foresight and willingness to break paradigms that had devastated Hungary.

Dr. Bánhegyi wanted to meet with us again two weeks later. At that initial meeting we were tasked with developing the following:

:: a curriculum writing plan

:: a plan to train, support and problem solve with teachers that would use our curriculum nationwide

:: a name for the nationwide movement we were hoping to become

:: dates for our first symposium to train the teachers in our curriculum

Before leaving we received vital research and sensitive documents outlining the social ills of Hungary. We also met and interviewed Dr. Szabó, the Head of Psychiatry at the hospital who was responsible for counseling AIDS patients. She was very concerned for the youth in Hungary and encouraged us to join in the fight.

We left the hospital, got in our car and drove away praising God. We prayed all the way back to my office. As soon as we arrived, we were greeted by many of our staff who had been praying for us. I formed a task force of five people and we immediately went to work.

After outlining our goals for the next two weeks and making responsibilities clear, we spent the next two weeks working like never before. We worked two consecutive 90-hour work weeks. Yet, the Lord kept us refreshed. We felt carried.

By the time we had to make our presentation to NEVI, we were ready. We had done our research and had great plans and material to present. But we had reason to believe that our two-week investment preparing for the meeting could lead to nothing.

:: The Birth of Youth at the Threshold of Life (YTL)::

(February 1994)

"The king's heart is a stream of water in the hand of the Lord;
he turns it wherever he will."

—Proverbs 21:1

T he day we'd anticipated and worked toward for two long weeks finally came—the meeting with NEVI. Gábor and I returned to the St. László Hospital with two briefcases loaded with research, curriculum outlines, videos and graphs. Dr. Bánhegyi and his team were waiting. After offering us coffee, Dr. Bánhegyi quickly opened the meeting with, *"Show us what you've got."*

We were ready. I spoke in English and Hungarian. Our young and talented staff, Gábor Grész, offered his translating help to me at very strategic moments. He also added key insight as I went through our team's presentation.

Dr. Bánhegyi said nothing the entire time. He listened respectfully and studied our material.

I first outlined our goals. Our curriculum would target the following among 13-16 year olds:

1. Increase the student's capacity to make friends by building their self-esteem, self-confidence and communication skills.

2. Decrease sexual promiscuity, sexually transmitted diseases (STDs), teen-age pregnancies and AIDS.

3. Increase understanding of the dangers of drugs and decrease drug abuse and first time drug usage.

4. Prepare them for adulthood, marriage and family by helping to strengthen their moral foundations, value system and character development.

Outside of these, we had the following goals for educators:

1. Refine the educator's teaching skills, helping them create an interactive classroom environment.

2. Train the educator to effectively and confidently teach the sensitive topics that our curriculum would address: sex, dating, marriage, values and character development, sexually transmitted diseases, drugs, etc.

As I spoke, the three women on NEVI's team looked back at me stoically. Every once in a while they would look over at Dr. Bánhegyi. None of them, not once during the entire presentation, said a single word. I asked if they had any questions throughout, but no one spoke. Dr. Bánhegyi simply waved me on. He wanted me to continue.

Next, I mentioned our training and delivery options. To train and support educators, we would utilize symposiums and regional meetings and form, as well as qualify, a "Guest Lecture Traveling Team" to handle special assemblies nationwide. I explained English summer camp opportunities for the students, too. We had a two-year plan ready, along with a budget. We talked through all of it. We also mentioned that we thought this program would become a nationwide movement if we delivered a great product.

I then came to a very sensitive topic. NEVI had posters up all over the city encouraging kids to use condoms. One of their sponsors was LifeStyle Condoms. They had given tons of money to NEVI. This meant that as one of NEVI's sponsors, LifeStyle Condoms would get good advertising nationwide for youth to use their product. This not-so-subtle message encouraged young people to have sex, too. This had to be addressed before we could partner with NEVI.

Whenever a LifeStyle Condom ad was on display—on television, in the newspaper or on a billboard—NEVI's logo was always beside it. If Campus Crusade was to partner with NEVI, we had to have a disclaimer anytime their logo was next to ours in the future, because we did not believe in that particular message. NEVI, our partner-to-be, obviously supported condom use. In our curriculum we were going to emphasize waiting to have sex until marriage and to abstain from sex until then. We were going to teach that condoms were unreliable.

I took a deep breath and shot up a prayer.

As I mentioned this concern, they remained silent. There were no objections. No cursing was hurled our way. Yet, there was no encouragement either. They seemed unmoved.

I went on to another sensitive topic—the most important one. As missionaries and ordained ministers, we had to have the Gospel in the curriculum. As communicators who valued connecting with others creatively, we did not have any desire or compulsion to be overly religious. We wanted to meet the needs NEVI identified among the youth authentically, yet knew students' deepest needs could not be met apart from Christ.

As I prepared for this second meeting, the Lord led me to the words He wanted me to use regarding this sensitive topic. I said, *"Dr. Bánhegyi, meeting these needs—the need for friendship, a healthy self-esteem, and building values and character to help prevent today's youth from falling into dangerous behaviors—we feel it is important to emphasize the ethics taught by Jesus Christ, Judeo-Christian ethics, and the relevance of a personal relationship with Him. These are Hungary's best moral traditions."*

There. I said it. I was almost finished with my presentation. They continued to sit in silence.

During the entire presentation, because of their silence, I said more than once to God, *"Well, that was a fun two weeks. I wonder why You had us do that, Lord."* I thought this plan of ours had more than a good chance of being rejected.

The Lord led us to save the name of the program and curriculum for the very end. *"We think the name of this program and curriculum should be called 'Youth at the Threshold of Life.'"*

Just as I said that, Dr. Bánhegyi was called into another office to answer an urgent fax. He left the room abruptly without saying a word to any of us. I looked at my watch. One hour and fifty minutes had passed.

Every once in a while during that lengthy time, I thought I detected slight smiles, but as I mentioned, no one said a word. It was quiet except for the sound of my voice. Yet, that changed when he left the room.

Immediately, the women in the room said, *"Oh, he loves this!"* Encouraged, I returned, *"Are you sure? He has not said anything and has practically sat motionless the entire time."* They replied, *"That is how we know he loves it. He is a very smart man and knows what he wants. If he didn't like it, he would have thrown you out within ten minutes."* I hoped they were right.

When Dr. Bánhegyi returned, he remained standing. I rose. A desk was between us. Immediately, he extended his right hand toward me and said, *"Excellent. I want to be your partner!"* As we shook hands he committed $20,000 to the initial project right then and there.

This was the beginning of a miracle. To this day we still cannot fully comprehend its impact. A simple letter requesting funds to buy a computer opened a door for incredible ministry.

:: Éva Mergl Remembers ::

H er parents left Hungary after the 1956 Hungarian Revolution failed to oust the Russian Soviets. After a brief stint in Germany, Éva and her family finally made their way to the USA. America became their new home. When she grew up and became a Christian, God called her back to Hungary.

Éva Mergl is a colleague of ours on staff with Campus Crusade for Christ in Hungary. She made special contributions to the first three editions of the *Youth at the Threshold of Life* (YTL) curriculum. Her creative, God-given gifts were put to great use on the very first day of the YTL miracle. On the day when Paul, Gábor and I returned from our initial meeting with Dr. Bánhegyi, Éva was the one who came up with the name. She burst into our office after one hour and said, *"I've got the name. We should call it 'Youth at the Threshold of Life.'"[3]* We immediately loved it.

Éva was there at the beginning, too—when, long before YTL, God had us at another threshold. She was a staff member in 1989 and remembers the difficulties we encountered in ministry. She was there when God taught us that He wanted us to go forward in His harvest on our knees.

---

3. Youth at the Threshold of Life has become more than a curriculum—it is a movement. See Appendix for more details.

She writes:

"I remember that nothing was working. There was disunity on the team and we were discouraged. We looked at the legend of the curse put on Hungary by the invading Mongols centuries ago. They hexed Hungary by sending evil spirits of fear, disunity and hopelessness. These were the very things we were struggling against in the ministry!

It made sense to take spiritual warfare seriously, as it was the key to overcoming in battle! Even though we were busy in ministry that time of the year, I remember setting aside a big chunk of time—a whole month – for prayer, fasting and studying the Word of God. It was so worth it!!!! As we began practicing the things we talked about and learned in Bible study, God began opening doors! The bondage and obstacles seemed to become less formidable and there was spiritual breakthrough in ministry.

Soon after, the YTL opportunity jumped out of nowhere. We were able to see it as an opportunity and be used by God as a tool to get His Word out to thousands of students, educators and parents. In the beginning it felt like we were being carried on the wings of the Spirit every minute of every day—kind of like living the book of Acts! If our spiritual eyes would still have been blinded as they were before the concentrated time of making prayer a priority, we would not have seen or been able to take part in this amazing miracle—a miracle that is still going on today, two decades later."

:: A Bizarre Path ::

(1994)

"A gift opens the way for the giver and ushers him
into the presence of the great."

—Proverbs 18:16

After our second meeting with NEVI, Gábor and I immediately went to work on research, writing and editing. We knew that the success of Youth at the Threshold of Life (YTL) hinged on quality curriculum. After all, ineffective curriculum is why Dr. Bánhegyi and NEVI were looking for new partners. We prayed and worked with focused discipline, enjoying God's grace as we went forward. The entire process of publishing the first edition took eleven months.

We had a great team of people helping. Éva Mergl, Edit Ficzere, Scott Neel, Edina Grész, Dan LaGue and Helen Filby formed the core of the team. Researchers and ministries from Atlanta, Colorado Springs, Dallas, Austin and foreign places like Malawi and India chipped in, too, with vitally important information. The more we planned for the future of YTL, the more budget needs grew. So, the team went to work on securing finances as well.

We hosted a trial symposium in Budapest from March 24-26, 1994 to test our material as we were writing and editing the first edition of YTL. We invited 130 previously disgruntled educators from multiple public schools from five different cities to join us for a special weekend. They had worked with NEVI before and formed the source of a nationwide complaint against Dr. Bánhegyi's office for squandering government money while wasting it on terrible curriculum.

God surprised us that weekend. As we taught, held seminars and spoke with others in private meetings, we discovered that they not only loved our curriculum plans, they loved us and wanted to lend a hand to make YTL a success.

Relieved, Dr. Bánhegyi dedicated himself to promoting YTL nationwide. Between March and December 1994, our ministry and YTL were ushered into the center of a nationwide news blitz that bombarded the Hungarian society with the cause of YTL.

During those months, Gábor and I locked in. We focused almost entirely on research and writing. We read everything we could get our hands on regarding AIDS, sexually transmitted diseases and educational philosophy. We studied the Word, prayed and wrote about friendship, self-worth, values and more. Creative energy surged. We scheduled regular times with each other and the team to review, edit and test our every thought. Our wives helped, too. Karen edited practically everything I wrote and Edina spent weeks translating everything into Hungarian once I was finished writing. This was a huge undertaking.

It affected our home life in humorous ways. At times, of course, I would talk with Karen about what we were writing. We discussed AIDS, sexually transmitted diseases and the global HIV epidemic in our home—not our typical conversations.

Our son Dan was nine years old at the time. One day, he pulled his mom aside.

"Mom, is sex a bad word?" Dan asked.

"No, honey, not at all." Karen replied. She then explained one meaning of the word sex was to differentiate between boys and girls, and then mentioned that I would soon be explaining to him the other way to define it.

"So, it is not a bad word, right?" Dan returned after Karen's explanation. Again, she said that it was not.

Dan was relieved. He then said, *"Well that's good, because Dad has sure been talking about sex a lot lately!"*

Later in the fall of 1994, as we were finishing the curriculum, another funny conversation occurred at the dinner table. Abbie was twelve years old. Dan had just turned ten. Katie was a wee six-year-old.

As we were having dinner, I was helping Dan study for a science test. He had to know the meaning of zygote, sperm, fertilization, the female egg, etc. You can imagine the raised eyebrows of a ten-year-old boy, the turned up smiles of an older sister and the sometimes breathless caution of a mom during that conversation.

What was Katie doing? I didn't notice.

While helping Dan study, I told him that we needed to have "the talk" soon. We had discussed sex very briefly in a private conversation just two weeks earlier.

Dan said, *"The talk?"*

I returned, *"You know—the talk..."* Then I whispered not so silently, *"...about sex."* Katie heard me. She then piped up innocently with her little girl voice. *"I know what sex is!"*

We all looked at each other. Karen smiled. I did, too.

Dan immediately said, *"Katie, you don't either! You don't know what sex is."*

Wanting to encourage Katie (and the conversation) I said, *"Well, Dan, maybe she does. Katie, what is sex?"*

All eyes were glued on Katie. We didn't have to wait for her response. She replied rather confidently, *"It's a disease."* She elongated the ease part of the last word. It was hilarious.

While we were writing YTL, Dr. Bánhegyi was promoting it. He put YTL in various news periodicals, including the prestigious medical journal known as *Catedra*. He also arranged interviews and documentaries on television and radio. He was very proud of the momentum he was creating for YTL nationwide.

It was already a bizarre path, but just as momentum was building, that path took a turn into darkness. Along a corridor on the YTL path, we encountered a looming obstacle that threatened to shut the whole thing down.

:: The AIDS Benefit Party in the Castle of Budapest ::

(October 1994)

"It is not those who are healthy who need a physician, but those who are sick; I did not come to call the righteous, but sinners."

—Jesus in Mark 2:17

We were invited to a special party by Dr. Bánhegyi. It was actually more than a party and more than an invitation. In his YTL promotion frenzy, Dr. Bánhegyi managed to secure us a prominent place at a prestigious benefit. Many politicians and businesses united for the purpose of throwing a "Ball" to benefit the Hungarian AIDS Foundation. It was held on October 28, 1994 in the Castle of Budapest.

Alongside the many festivities, three organizations were selected to educate the guests regarding needs surrounding the global AIDS crisis and its current threat to Hungary. These organizations were given beautiful exhibit space in the castle, along with banners to advertise themselves to those at the party. The three organizations chosen for exhibits were: International Red Cross, Hungarian AIDS Foundation and Campus Crusade for Christ.

This was more than an honor. It was an open door that would give YTL great exposure.

Gábor and I were asked to attend a pre-party planning two weeks prior to the benefit. We went. As we toured the castle and found out more about the program, without speaking to each other, we both were feeling like this party might not be such a good idea. We discovered the following at that planning meeting:

:: A provocative drawing of a naked woman, from her belly button to the top of her knees, was front and center on the posters and tickets promoting the event.

:: People of questionable moral character and divergent sexual practices were leading the committee to organize the event.

:: They expected 4,000 of the highest in society to be there.

:: The following would be part of the program:

... free champagne and vodka would flow from 7:00 p.m. to 3:00 a.m.

... four rock and jazz bands would perform

... four different fashion shows were to be held, including one that would promote very provocative lingerie

... a disco would begin at midnight

... a trip to Crete was to be the raffle prize

... free watches, condoms, Pepsi, cell phones and t-shirts were to be given out

All of this together felt very dark to us. No one knew it, but we were feeling uneasy as we left the pre-party planning. Troubled, we headed to my apartment and began to talk about what we should do.

We prayed. We questioned. We deliberated. Gábor and I were confused. On the one hand, it was going to be a party that would make my college fraternity parties seem like Vacation Bible School. There was going to be immorality, money and liquor flowing all night long. On the other hand, Dr. Bánhegyi may not have understood had we declined this invitation. We feared that he or NEVI might write us off as religious bigots if we refused to go to the party.

None of that mattered deep down. We just wanted to know what to do.

The whole ministry knew of the pre-party planning. All of us were reeling with joy and surprise at the favor God was giving us in the eyes of so many people. This was His doing, so all of us, in a spirit of humble fear, sought the Lord daily. We were taking everything to Him in prayer.

That's what Gábor and I were doing as we sat in the living room of my apartment. We were also seriously considering calling Dr. Bánhegyi with the news that we would not be attending.

Just then, Karen walked in with groceries in her hands and asked, *"Well, how did it go?"* We told her. We told her about the type of people planning the benefit and how they seemed more interested in the party than in the party's so-called "cause." We told her of the nude promotional pieces, the party favors, the program—we told her everything. We told her we did not think we should go, and what a dilemma it was for us in our relationship with Dr. Bánhegyi. He was so excited to promote YTL and was doing us so many favors.

She said something and then went into the kitchen to unpack her groceries. Gábor and I went back to prayer.

Karen returned within one minute, uncharacteristically interrupted our prayer, and asked us a very important question—a question that both rebuked and rocked us. With eyes wide open in excitement she asked, *"Would Jesus go to the party?"*

Immediately we knew. Gábor and I looked at each other and almost simultaneously said, *"We are going!"* Karen went on to say that the Lord had given her a verse that she thought was for us at this very moment. She then read Mark 2:15-17.

"And it happened that He was reclining at the table in his house, and many tax collectors and sinners were dining with Jesus and His disciples; for there were many of them, and they were following Him. When the scribes of the Pharisees saw that He was eating with the sinners and tax collectors, they said to His disciples, 'Why is He eating and drinking with tax collectors and sinners?' And hearing this, Jesus said to them, 'It is not those who are healthy who need a physician, but those who are sick; I did not come to call the righteous, but sinners.' "

With great confidence that the Lord Himself would have gone, we went to the AIDS Benefit two weeks later.

We were invited to the AIDS Benefit because of the success Youth at the Threshold of Life had enjoyed up until that moment in time. Ironically, we had neither a curriculum, nor had yet to train even one educator. But God made sure that YTL was well-promoted for reasons only He knew. We were on TV and in the newspapers. Many government, educational and AIDS activist organizations were very interested in YTL. Momentum was growing.

To prepare for the party we prayed a lot. We also assembled a team of staff and students to craft our exhibit, and trained students how to share the Gospel at the party.

During the AIDS Benefit, thousands of elegantly dressed people from high society visited each of the three exhibits. All three were artistically arranged in a beautiful part of the castle. We were very pleased with our location. The party planning team set us up very well to promote YTL.

Our exhibit included an awesome display of our YTL banner and slogan, pictures of young people, quotes by history's best educators, endorsements from famous people in Hungary, books and colorful brochures. We displayed what we could of our curriculum, too. At that very time the publishers were printing the YTL curriculum for a symposium deadline. Our first YTL Symposium was about one month away.

This may sound a bit cocky, but of the three exhibits, we think ours was the best. It was so attractive that many who walked through lingered to talk about our new program. Our student leaders and staff looked great, and were friendly and knowledgeable hosts.

Visiting us that night were famous TV and film actors, educators, poets and politicians. We had approximately 500 people visit us. About 100 of them took Gospel literature and 20 more heard the Gospel one-on-one. One woman I shared the Gospel with at the party that night met with one of our staff twice for follow-up and later joined a small group Bible study. Outside of that, many key contacts were made to expand the ministry audience of YTL and further publicize our curriculum and events.

Thousands came to the AIDS Benefit that night. It was wild and worldly. Everybody was unbelievably decked out. It was high society doing some low-life living, but it was also wonderful. Like Jesus often did, we crashed the party, compelled by His love for the "*sick and the sinning.*"

:: The AIDS Convention ::

(November 17-18, 1994)

"But the Lord said to me, "Do not say, 'I am only a child.' You must go to everyone I send you to and say whatever I command you. Do not be afraid of them, for I am with you and will rescue you," declares the Lord."

—Jeremiah 1:7-8

Preceding World AIDS Day in December, NEVI planned a nationwide AIDS Convention in late November. Eighty-five speakers were selected to discuss the most pertinent social, medical, educational and emotional issues related to HIV. It was an impressive line-up. Speakers included politicians, medical professionals, military doctors, university professors, and pharmaceutical personnel.

Dr. Bánhegyi invited me to be the sole foreigner to address the conference and slated me for a morning session on the first day. I was invited to speak on *"Education Beyond Sex"* and to introduce *"Youth at the Threshold of Life; a values and character-building, abstinence-based program for today's youth in Hungary."* After my speech, I was to moderate an open forum and participate on a panel designed to address issues related to my topic. The panel was to be a cross between a serious Q and A session and a debate. Joining me on the panel were six others: two from Parliament, two university professors and two doctors.

This was a radical opportunity for us! Are you grinning? Gábor and I did, too. We could not believe this was happening! At that time Bill Clinton was President of the United States of America and had a very liberal Surgeon General, Dr. Jocelyn Elders. Dr. Bánhegyi's invitation was like Dr. Elders inviting an evangelical to speak to the AIDS activists in America at a similar function.

The day of the AIDS Convention finally arrived. There were 500 educators, politicians and doctors attending the main session when I delivered my speech.

As I was introduced, it was immediately obvious that I was not Hungarian. My name and accent made sure of that. I stepped up to the microphone and began to speak. Of course, it was in Hungarian. This evidently surprised the audience. They burst into applause as I began talking. Stunned, I lapsed into terrible Hungarian for a brief moment, and then recovered (by the grace of God).

Afterwards, 150 at the convention attended my panel. I was nervous. I hoped that I had answers to any question they asked. I wondered if our position regarding waiting to have sex until marriage and being faithful in a monogamous relationship would be attacked. I would surely find out during the panel. Yet, all went well. People were pleased and challenged by the arguments I presented and the needs we were targeting in the YTL material.

I share this with you in the spirit of a little child filled with joy. To this day, I cannot believe God did that for our ministry. But He did. God was building momentum. He was tearing down the enemy's strongholds. He was preparing the way for His light to break through in a land where darkness had reigned for so long. Increasingly, it made sense to us that God wanted us to go through each door He opened with absolute humility. We knew it was His doing and we did not want to get in His way.

He was teaching us how to minister to others, too, as we went down this bizarre path. Bizarre? Well, yes. It was so, so new. We had no idea what we were doing. We simply prayed, worked hard, made sure we had good counsel and great resources, insisted on team unity and humbly proceeded down the road.

I wrote the following to our prayer and financial support team (those in America who sent us to Hungary) in November of 1994: *"We're working hard and praying a lot, but in a strange way we feel like God is simply moving in a very unusual way to accomplish plans that we can't yet fully comprehend."*

That is exactly how we felt. We were moving into new, uncharted territory, all the while experiencing great joy as God surprised us with so many open doors.

:: Momentum ::

By December 1994 the following had happened:

:: We made plans for Josh McDowell (author, speaker, apologist) to help us gain credibility and momentum with both educators and politicians, as well as to reach out to university students. (From February 26 - March 4, 1995, Josh not only spoke to thousands at various outreaches, but blessed the Body of Christ by helping us host a prayer conference for pastors and Christian leaders in Budapest. That week Josh also coached our staff regarding how to think about the opportunity that was unfolding for us with Youth at the Threshold of Life.)

:: NEVI gave us $20,000 to write the curriculum and host the March Symposium.

:: Dick Day, an educator from Malawi, spoke at our first symposium and mentored Gábor and me in writing, research and communication.

:: The largest cable TV network in Hungary interviewed us about YTL and put it in one million homes. They also broadcasted our videos on TV!

:: A director of five high schools expressed that she wanted YTL in all of her schools!

:: A Parent Teacher Association in Nyíregyháza, a city in Hungary, invited us to participate in discussions on sex and morals in education and to share our program with the educators of their city.

:: One of our staff in Szeged was asked to teach English in the university and was allowed to use *Youth at the Threshold of Life* as his curriculum!

:: The city of Győr requested a teachers training symposium.

:: Mission agencies wanted the training so they could use it in their ministries.

:: People from the cities of Eger and Kecskemét expressed interest in using YTL.

:: Twenty-four pastors met with us to hear about the YTL ministry opportunity and how they could use it for church growth and evangelism. Joining us were Reform (known as Presbyterians in the USA), Baptist, Pentecostal, Lutheran, Methodist and Inter-Varsity leaders. Their response was overwhelmingly positive and very encouraging! We prayed together for wisdom, protection and open doors. As a fairly young parachurch organization in Hungary we were profoundly blessed by these precious leaders.

The Lord protected us and provided for us all along the way.

:: YTL'S First Symposium and 'The Klára Profile' ::

(December 2-4, 1994)

"I know that You can do all things;
no plan of Yours can be thwarted."

—Job 42:2

T he time had come for our very first YTL Symposium. It was hosted at The Regina, a quaint hotel and conference center in Budafok, a suburb located in the south of Budapest's Buda side.

People from all over the country were anxious to come and be trained. We had hit on a need nerve. Most teachers could not believe that such a program existed.

A woman came to me on the second day of the training. As she approached, her humble demeanor revealed deep gratitude as tears filled her eyes. She thanked me for "allowing" her to be trained. In all, over 300 came for certification and training that weekend. One of them was Dr. Klára.

She was a pediatrician from the city of Csurgó and responsible for the health care in multiple public schools in her region. She was well-educated, influential and very dedicated. Yet, everything she learned at the YTL Symposium that weekend was new to her. Over the course of the weekend, a burden that made her weep and pound the table was developing in Klára's heart.

As she learned of the needs among our youth in Hungary, her burden became a radical plan. She took personal responsibility to new levels. Something had to be done. She could not sleep. Important values needed to be taught and modeled to our teens. Dangerous behaviors that young people were adopting had to stop.

After the symposium concluded, Dr. Klára went back to Csurgó with a plan. It was simple. Go to every bar in her city and get the attention of each bartender or owner.

After introducing herself, she would say to each one, *"Students and young people come in here and are introduced to alcohol and drugs. From here they go and have unprotected sex. There is a rise of sexually transmitted diseases in Hungary. A tide of immorality is sweeping our nation! And this very place and other places like this all across Hungary represent the very source of our problem."* She said this to every bartender and owner in five different establishments in her city.

Stunned, each and every last one of them stood motionless, transfixed by this little woman of great zeal. She continued. *"I insist, in the name of all that is good in Hungary and for the sake of our nation's future, that you show this video around the clock! The youth in our city must be exposed to this message!"*

She gave them each a video copy of No Second Chance. This video was part of our first two editions of YTL. No Second Chance has testimonial stories from people of all ages who contracted HIV. Their stories are well-told and heart-felt. No Second Chance also contains statistics and vital information about AIDS, sex, and STDs (sexually transmitted diseases). All of it is well-presented by doctors, nurses and health officials. There are also two stories of men who had placed their faith in Jesus, but eventually died of AIDS.

The bar owners did what Dr. Klára said to do. They showed the video. That meant the Gospel was going out with the endorsement of bartenders and was being viewed by everyone in their bars. Most of those people would never have stepped one foot into a church or gone to an outreach event, but God had inspired a little woman, who in turn inspired bartenders to share the Gospel via video in the bars of her town.

Klára had not been told to do this. None of us on the YTL team found out about Klára or her exploits until months after the symposium. But when we did, we were glad—very glad. This was a new work of God in our midst. We rejoiced. Klára became a regular at the symposium for the next two years. At each symposium she inspired her colleagues to take action.

Klára became a symbolic figure for Gábor and me. She represented the spirit of the YTL movement in every way. She became the model—the profile, if you will—of the educators that take our curriculum back to their schools and communities. There is nothing typical about these dear educators. Like Klára, they are unique. They all fit the following profile, the "Klára profile."

They are:

:: Intelligent. They are all well-educated, some with triple doctorates.

:: Compassionate and Passionate. The vast majority of all educators using YTL grew up and suffered under communism. They want the very best for this new generation! They are willing to take risks in expressing their concerns and willing to do anything to help today's youth in Hungary.

:: Non-believers. Yes, Klára did all of this as an atheist. In the first fifteen years, about 80% of all educators trained in YTL are non-Christians. Many of these educators return to symposiums year after year. After hearing the Gospel over and over again, many eventually come to Christ.

But what about Klára?

Klára dropped out of sight for about four years. Then in the spring of 2000 we received a letter from her husband, whom we had never met.

He wrote:

"Dear Friends of Timóteus Társaság,

It has been many years since Klára has attended your symposiums. Klára still uses the YTL curriculum faithfully in many schools. She also trains other doctors and educators to use it each and every year.

The main purpose of writing you today is to thank you.

Thank you for leading Klára to Christ. Two years after the first symposium she put her faith in Christ. Then she led me to Christ. This completely saved our marriage and family. Thank you. Thank you. Eventually we led our two sons to Christ, too. We study the Bible every week as a family and we have become active members in a great church.

There is so much more to tell you and we will. We plan to visit you on Saturday at your next symposium. We will be in Budapest and plan on dropping by. We have to see you and express our gratitude to you personally.

With friendship,

Tamás"

That happened six years after we began.

But for now, let's go back to December 1994. The first year of YTL was ending. How appropriate to finish the year exactly how it started. We headed right back to prayer. Our prayer emphasis in 1994 was filled with praise, thanksgiving and awe. It was easy to hit our knees. That is where we wanted to stay.

God was at work in a new way. We felt like the Lord was walking through the middle of Hungary with a determined stride, with joy in His eyes and a sure grin on His face! He had taken hold of us and said, *"Come on with me! I'm doing something here right now and I want you in on it. Be sure of this – I want it done and it will happen according to my desire. Nothing I want done can be thwarted."*

:: Paradigm Shift ::

(1995)

They were "praising God and enjoying the favor of all the people. And the Lord added to their number daily those who were being saved."

—Acts 2:47

YTL broke our ministry paradigm in every way.

Prayer was already in every fabric of our ministry, but we needed wisdom as never before—wisdom in handling the media and in networking with non-believers. We asked the corners of the globe to pray that our program would be in more high schools, for more students to receive Christ, that more would become His faithful disciples and that our budget would be better funded to take advantage of this incredible opportunity! We still beg God earnestly for all of these things.

But, beyond prayer, God wanted us to think and act differently as we reached out to the lost. In Campus Crusade we pride ourselves on taking the initiative. We believe that a friendly, simple, direct and conversationally mature proclamation of the Gospel is one of the most important, first steps in ministry.

Proclamation leads to eternal life. Sharing the truth of God's Word and the Gospel is the most relevant thing we can do.

Jesus promised that there is good soil out there. Good soil will respond. Bad soil will not. Good soil will respond to the Gospel—*eventually*. A great way to determine what good soil looks like is in John 3:21. Jesus promises that those who practice the truth will come to the light. In other words, those sincere seekers who are honest with the truth will respond. We don't have to work ourselves into a lather of relevance. We should sow it broadly and directly without fear or regret.

Don't get me wrong. Crusade loves relevance, creativity and tact. We just balance it all with trying to turn conversations to Christ as often and as soon as possible. Yet, when YTL entered our ministry and lives, God wanted us to learn more about sharing His heart with others in ways we had not experienced that deeply before.

There are those who weep that Jesus wants to weep with *through us*. There are those who are not yet saved, but are good-heartedly trying to make a difference in society that Jesus wants to help *through us*.

Not only does Jesus want to **proclaim** the Gospel through us, He also wants to **do good** things through us. Peter, as he was sharing the Gospel to the first Gentile, summarized Jesus' ministry this way:

> "The word which He sent to the sons of Israel, **preaching peace through Jesus Christ (He is Lord of all)** — you yourselves know the thing which took place throughout all Judea, starting from Galilee, after the baptism which John proclaimed. You know of Jesus of Nazareth, how God anointed Him with the Holy Spirit and with power, and how He went about **doing good** and healing all who were oppressed by the devil, for God was with Him."[4]

---

4. Acts 10:36-38

Doing good is part of a Gospel ministry. Proclamation is not enough. God wants to do good works through us. Good works must be viewed by the Church as important and valuable.

We are learning that presence and persuasion are essential, too. If we are present, actually with the people, we will learn their needs. If we reach out in love, doing the work of meeting those needs, persuasion of epic proportions will result. Persuasion happens because God's love is authentic. Persuasion is nothing more than God's love in motion. Being present long enough to learn the needs of others is the domino that sets dynamic persuasion in motion and leads to an exponentially broad proclamation of the Gospel!

There are two major spheres on this planet of ours and there are many ways to categorize those two spheres. For our purposes, let's identify them broadly as the "Church" and the "World." The usual interplay between these two spheres can be described this way:

> *The World never really moves in the direction of the Church,*
> *and the Church rarely moves in the direction of the World.*

The Church often tries to reach the World. And sometimes it does rather effectively. There are exceptions, but there are not enough of them. When the Church does move in that direction, the connection we obtain with the World never really lasts that long. It may last as long as a survey, a Gospel presentation or as long as an outreach event, followed by a conversation over coffee. The Church makes all kinds of connections with the World through church services, books and radio—it's just not for very long. We go. They listen; yet, never for very long. Then they either push back or we walk away. Relationally, the connection is typically not very strong.

After one year, the Youth at the Threshold of Life program really connected with the World. Non-Christian educators were calling us all the time to invite us to be guest lecturers in public schools. They would come to a part in the curriculum, the Christian part, and say things like, *"Um. I've come to the Jesus part during my classroom preparation. I can't teach this. Could you either come yourself or send someone to teach this with integrity? I sure hope you can."*

Non-believers were calling to invite us to share the Gospel in their classrooms. That has consistently happened for over fifteen years and continues to this day.

The two circles below represent the two spheres—the Church and the World. It may help to keep in mind that the YTL Team (staff and missionaries with Crusade, church volunteers from hundreds of churches, etc.) is on the left. Non-believing educators in a post-communist nation are on the right.

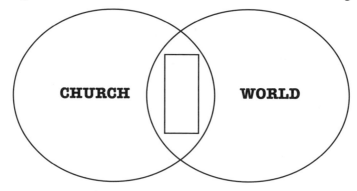

By listening to Dr. Bánhegyi and the educators, the YTL Team discovered the felt needs of the World. Parents, politicians, educators and the medical world were focused on youth problems. We entered their world. We studied their needs. We began to share their agenda. We had similar burdens. The youth had to be helped. We asked God to help us meet their needs; needs for curriculum, youth clubs, parent-teacher communication, along with educator training and support. As bond-servants of Christ, we were careful to never compromise the Gospel when meeting those needs. We shared it as often, and as clear and direct as possible. They knew we were Christians from the get-go.

We listened. We offered to help. The World responded. Some called us "AIDS Activists." We let them. To this day, some respond to the Gospel and some do not. Some use the Gospel in our curriculum (71%) and some do not. But every last one of them stays connected to us. They call us. They come back to everything we invite them to. They host us in their towns. They send us birthday cards. They ask for our autographs. They cry with us. They laugh with us. They disagree with us. But they lock arms with us because we are mutually committed to the cause of helping youth.

Referring to the circle diagram on the previous page, it is as though they come to a window, peer in and say, *"You all are Christians? I'm surprised."*

If that box in the center can be referred to as a window for the World, it is definitely a door for the Body of Christ. We have walked through that door for over 15 years. On the other side of that door are great people – people in all segments of society – who are opening doors, creating opportunities and partnering with us.

At the door they say to us over and over again: *"You are helping me." "You met a need." "I like this." "I'm changing into a better person because of you."*

Often something extraordinary happens. It is for these moments we endure. Some say,

> *"You gave me the truth in love. I repent. I believe. I place my trust in Jesus. I want to dedicate myself to the highest cause of this movement – following Jesus and helping others come to know Him."*

Why this surprising reaction? Why are the World and the Church getting along so well, without the Church compromising the Gospel?

The quick answer is the most profound answer – it is the grace of God. Yet, there are practical principles that can be studied and applied. I'll list two here, but more will be discussed later.

:: Love ::

Love is the key. Jesus loved like no other. He wants to express His love through us.

One day, Jesus was walking through Jericho, looked up at a person of the World and said, *"Zaccheus, I must stay at your house today."* What motivated

Jesus to use the word *"must"*? It was love. It was a deeply felt, very sincere love. And that love changed Zaccheus. He repented of defrauding others and Jesus declared that *"salvation has come to this house."* Luke 19:1-10 describes the whole story.

Jesus' love through us says, *"I must. I must love. I must meet needs."*

People who are privately suffering will respond to authentic people who show they can relate to their world. They will wait in line saying, "Influence me!" to people who understand, who confront without pushing, who relate to them authentically. If they are leaders, like those connected to us in YTL, they will walk with you for a long, long time if you produce something they need that is excellent, intriguing and smart.

That leads us to the second lesson we learned.

:: Excellence and a Good Name ::

In Acts 2:47 the early church had *"the favor of all the people."* How did this come about? We surmise, as we look back at the history of YTL, that it had something to do with love and truth being lived out as the Church rubbed shoulders with the World.

As we have done that, as we have loved them and spoken the truth, God in His grace has allowed us to gain a good name.

We feel that we are stewards of the lessons we are learning. As we've moved forward, we desire that love be authentically communicated in word and deed. We have also insisted on excellence in execution across the board.

Solomon wrote, *"A good name is more desirable than great riches; to be esteemed is better than silver or gold."*[5]

A good name is important. It is not important enough to compromise our faith, doctrine or obedience to Jesus. That much is clear. Yet it plays an important role for YTL.

---

5. Proverbs 22:1

Everyone on a ministry team has the power to help you develop and maintain a good reputation. As each member commits to the mission and values of the team, they must be held accountable to excellent execution. Commitment to excellence and accountability helps build a good name and a good reputation. When done, trust and confidence emerge from those you help. And that is a very good thing. It honors Jesus.

First impressions last. Never forget that. We remember God impressing upon us the need for His wisdom and self-control when we began YTL. Each time we met with a government leader, the media or an educator we asked God for help. Why? We wanted to make a great first impression.

Many have asked us, *"How do you introduce your program to community leaders?"* It is a good question. What you say at the beginning is important. It has to be brief and well-communicated. Keep in mind it may open or close a door.

We say something like the following:

"We are committed to developing youth through effective relationship and character development-based education while emphasizing the Judeo-Christian ethics taught by Jesus and the relevance of a relationship with him.

Youth at the Threshold of Life has multi-faceted programs that contribute to the lives of middle and high school students, educators and other professionals working directly with students. We seek to care for and resource them in such a way as to help them grow personally and professionally – helping them to balance all dimensions of life while emphasizing the spiritual area."

Love keeps it real. Excellence keeps it working.

Section Seven

:: Take Jesus to School ::

:: Take Jesus to School - 'TJTS' ::

(1996 - 1999)

*What would you say about God if He provided a way
for a ministry to teach public school teachers to share
Christ in public classrooms in former communist
nations with the backing of the government?*

Memories tell us that every moment in life is potentially meaningful. The moments we choose to remember are those key memories from the deep places where our soul's best treasures are kept!

God places a huge importance on the worshipful act of remembering what He has done. For example, the Israelites witnessed a great miracle of God when He divided the waters of the Jordan just as Joshua was leading them into the Promised Land. After over forty years of waiting, you would imagine that many in the crowd would be tempted to hastily keep going. Before moving on, however, God had them stop and remember. In Joshua 4:5-7 we read that God asked them to place a stone for each tribe taken from the middle of the Jordan (the place of the miracle) and fix it in a place they could come back to.

"Let this be a sign among you, so that when your children ask later, saying, 'What do these stones mean to you?' then you shall say to them, 'Because the waters of the Jordan were cut off before the ark of the covenant of the LORD; when it crossed the Jordan, the waters of the Jordan were cut off.' So these stones shall become a memorial to the sons of Israel forever."

Remembering God's work is important.

As YTL grew, we felt the Lord stressing upon us the importance of remembering Him and His works.

The YTL movement grew very quickly. It went to all corners of the Hungarian nation. It was truly a work of God. By the summer of 1996, just 18 months after beginning, our YTL curriculum was being taught in 79 cities by 870 educators, doctors and health officials, military chaplains, social workers, parents and community leaders. Of the 870 using YTL, 653 were educators and teachers from 400 different high schools.

At that time it was endorsed and used by the following:

:: NEVI and the National AIDS Coordinator

:: Directors of the Center for Disease Control representing many Hungarian counties

:: County educational superintendents

:: Over 400 local high school principals and over 650 teachers

:: County Health and Nurse Associations throughout Hungary

:: The Director of the Hungarian Army Chaplains

:: Church leaders throughout Hungary

Enthusiastic endorsements demonstrated early on that God intended to sweep the nation with the Gospel through YTL. Here are a few comments from those who backed YTL:

"This is not only an AIDS prevention program, nor only a sexual health program. It shows young people how to live."

—Dr. Dénes Bánhegyi, AIDS Coordinator

"There is an enormous responsibility on our shoulders because we have something in our hands that would be a sin not to pass on."

—T. Agnes, nurse

"I've found good solutions to very real needs. I like this program a lot."

—F. Attila, student

"This program is for the future of mankind. It is clear, teachable, draws attention and is sometimes shocking. This is the only way that seems to really work."

—I. Péter, teacher

"This is the kind of education that tries to achieve positive changes, not only in physical behavior, but also in spiritual life (moral values and character), and because of this, is much more effective and has better results."

—K. Márta, teacher

YTL was, and still is, a very special stone of memorial for all of us.

Even though we had barely begun this new ministry, God was preparing to challenge us to pioneer something new again. There was another moment ready to dawn upon all of us. It is a moment that we will never forget. It is one of our family's and ministry's few stones of memorial that we are sure God would have us remember for the rest of our lives and teach to our children. This new special moment started in 1996 and lasted through June of 1999. It was another miracle of God's choosing. You can see His glory in it.

The moment includes an incredible opportunity, great angst, a vision and a specific strategy.

:: Opportunity ::

In August of 1996, Tamás Heizer and Paul Held, two church planting missionaries in Hungary, were in our office purchasing some books and discipleship material.

Tamás said to me, *"Have you heard about the new law?"* I had not.

The government was fed up. The fall of communism occurred in 1989. Since then, there was an ever growing problem in the public school system. Educational standards and accountability were lacking. From 1989-1996 things in Hungary changed rapidly and often. Democracy was young. Freedoms were being discovered and tested. In the world of education, things were getting out of hand.

Earlier that spring, the Hungarian Ministry of Education pushed a new law through the Parliament. They enacted the National Curriculum Act. It was to be ratified two years later in the fall of 1998. They wanted to give all school districts in Hungary enough time to implement this new law because it would bring radical change in every department, every budget and every school.

The law included an unusual mandate. In the history section of the National Curriculum Act it stated that by the time a student was 16 years old, he or she had to know *"the essentials of Christianity and the New Testament."* After 40 years of communistic-atheism, the country was re-examining its Christian heritage and was looking for its moral soul.

They now required that students learn about the life of Jesus Christ, general facts about Christianity and how the Church grew throughout the world. It listed New Testament characters, places, events and concepts like Pontius Pilate, Mary, Joseph, Bethlehem, the Apostles, Messiah, Redeemer and Golgotha.

Look at that list again. The more we did, we came to believe that the Holy Spirit must have had a myriad of angels all over the legislators when they chose that list of words. We thought, *"How could you teach those things without sharing the Gospel of our Lord Jesus Christ?"*

This law had to be fulfilled in a history class, or should the teacher decide, in a President's Class (similar to homeroom classes in the USA). This meant it affected each school and every child in the nation in those schools: approximately 700,000 students in more than 4,500 schools. All schools had until the fall of 1998 to create and approve curriculum plans that fulfilled the law.

Every school had to make many adjustments. This frustrated educators and parents alike. It was a perfect time to introduce a new curriculum.

:: Angst ::

It may surprise you, but this new law brought great angst. Something had to be done, but we were very tired as a ministry. There were so many wonderful opportunities within YTL and campus ministry. We felt we were almost drowning—in way over our heads already. Besides, our YTL and Community Ministry Teams were understaffed. It was hard to imagine taking on another curriculum project.

Burdened, we started encouraging other ministries to write a curriculum to take advantage of the new law. This was to no avail. Each ministry leader said the same thing, *"You do it. Timóteus Társaság should do it. You all have the resources, momentum and reputation. You are known by many of the schools already through YTL. The credibility you have will open the door for all of us – the whole Body of Christ."*

But I did not want to. It made no sense to me. We were tired from writing and editing our second edition of YTL. We were pressing forward on a new front for YTL to mobilize church volunteers to be guest lecturers. We were also writing YTL Club material for various venues afforded by the open doors nationwide. The new law presented another unique open door, but leading the way through this threshold would have to come from somewhere else—writing a new curriculum and creating a new plan was simply out of the question for us.

The Lord, however, had other plans. He would not let this go. A very strong impression continued to bombard my mind and disturb my heart for weeks. A voice in my head kept saying, *"This cannot be ignored!"*

My angst was deep and personal. I could not shake these thoughts,

> *"If the Body of Christ does not do something soon, then some Fifth Avenue New York publisher will create a curriculum and secure a nationwide contract. If that happens, they will redefine who Jesus is and the opportunity for sharing the Gospel will be lost.*
>
> *We have a very short window of time. What if Parliament rescinds this law and they change their minds?" (Things like that happened all the time as Hungary was moving into democracy.)*

On top of that, in my personal times with the Lord, I struggled in prayer with thoughts about how to mobilize the church. We had learned a lot about mobilization, yet with the huge opportunity YTL gave us, we had only successfully trained 80 to be guest lecturers to help take advantage of the open doors YTL provided.

:: More Angst ::

> *"How can the Church be mobilized nationwide to run through this wide open door? The National Curriculum Act is a miracle, but what can we really do?"*

Honestly, for about three weeks these thoughts filled me with so much concern I could not stop talking, thinking and praying about it. It was strange. Deep within me, I wanted to walk away from it. I was feeling overwhelmed and did not want to pioneer another new project. However, God did not allow these thoughts to go away. It felt as though I was held captive. The burden of these thoughts—the angst—seemed to fuel my prayer and thought life.

:: Vision ::

I will never forget September 9, 1996.

Unexpectedly, during my normal time of prayer, as I was praying for wisdom about what to do regarding the National Curriculum Act, the most unusual thing that has ever happened to me occurred.

As I wrestled before God, asking Him to mobilize His Church and seeking Him for what we should do, a "vision" came. The vision was more of an emotional visionary picture, but it came with words, too. I began to write down my thoughts. Thoughts were coming quickly. It was as though all that gave angst, the burden of all my thoughts from the previous three weeks, began to be lifted as I turned toward this vision. The visionary picture included an event for the purpose of training and prayer. As I thought about this, my heart began to hope that mobilizing the Church was possible. The event I was picturing had to be led by people who were evangelists. Those people had to have the following convictions based on their experience with the Lord:

:: The sins of the nation must be confessed and Satan must be resisted!

:: God answers prayer!

:: Evangelism works because the Gospel is the power of God for salvation!

:: God wants to use you and me mightily for His glory!

God was telling me that Timóteus Társaság was to hold a training and prayer event led by spiritual leaders who could say all of those things from their hearts and lives. There was to be no compromise in this.

:: Strategy ::

These simple thoughts grabbed me. I wrote all of them down. As I went to the office that day, I asked the JESUS Film Team, Community Team and YTL Team to meet. I shared the vision with them. They responded with words of affirmation, wisdom and enthusiasm. That day we began to strategize. Within two weeks we had a plan that would soon take our ministry to new frontiers. That plan was affectionately known as Take Jesus to School[1] (TJTS).

Here is the gist of the plan we felt God would have us pursue.

1. We would write a curriculum that would take up three history class periods only. The last class period would include the part in the JESUS Film which captures the Lord's Supper, the death and resurrection of Jesus

---

1. Vidd Jézust az Iskolába in Hungarian

Christ and presents the Gospel. At the end of the film an opportunity is given to turn to Jesus in faith and receive Him as Lord and Savior.

2. We would host highly visionary training events. Those events were to be led by leaders experienced in prayer and evangelism. The vision I had received made that very clear. In order to mobilize the Church to *"take Jesus to schools,"* they had to be led by these kinds of leaders.

3. Each trained volunteer was to approach two to five school principals and present to them a *"Research Trial Offer."* They were to say, *"We represent Timóteus Társaság, the foundation who created Youth at the Threshold of Life. We would like to offer you a new curriculum to help you accomplish one of the history requirements outlined in the National Curriculum Act. We would like to have the best quality curriculum by the year 1998 when the law must be ratified. If you agree to help us by using the curriculum and having teachers and students evaluate it, we will give you 150 copies of the student book—the book of Luke (which included an article by Bill Bright and a Gospel presentation), three copies of the JESUS Film on video, and three copies of the teacher's manual for free. All you have to do is use it and then evaluate it."*

4. If the school chose to participate, the volunteer would then return to the school at the agreed upon time to collect the evaluations, build relationships, invite them to participate in a YTL Symposium and try to secure a YTL Club for students in their school.

This was the plan, but would it work? Ask yourself this: *"Would it work in your country?"* Go ahead and muse on that. It will help you glorify God with us regarding what He did in Hungary.

To make a long and glorious story short, here is what happened through TJTS:

1. By October 1996 three volunteers wrote a very professional curriculum within three weeks of me sharing the vision. It is called *"Educational*

Supplement: Christianity's Origin, The New Testament and The Life of Jesus." It was written by Attila Varga (a YTL and JESUS Film volunteer who was also a high school history teacher), Zsolt Kompán (JESUS Film Team member) and his wife Júlia Kompán. They worked together very well and very quickly. Imagine, one Baptist (Atilla) and two Presbyterians (Zsolt and Júlia) joining together to move the Kingdom forward! These were the first fruits of mobilizing the Body of Christ in Hungary.

2. By December 1996, ten staff test-marketed the idea and it was a huge success.

3. By October of 1997, we had hosted two trainings that emphasized prayer, fasting and evangelism training. There were 1,100 mobilized to Take Jesus to School. We had never seen anything like this before. It truly was a work of God and shows what great things can happen when the Body of Christ decides to work together.

4. In the spring of 1998 the newly elected administration in the Hungarian Government rescinded the National Curriculum Act. It was no longer necessary to teach Jesus or Christianity in school, but by then the momentum of TJTS was unstoppable.

5. In the summer of 1998 Zsolt Kompán, one of the authors of the TJTS curriculum and valuable team member, suddenly died of a brain aneurysm. God had graciously chosen and wonderfully used Zsolt to make a very significant contribution at the very end of his life.

6. By May 1999 the Take Jesus to School miracle made such a profound impact in Hungarian schools that it continues to amaze us to this day. From November 1996 to May 1999, TJTS saw the following:

   :: 1,107 volunteers were trained from 58 churches.

   :: TJTS volunteers went to every single public school with the offer to use our curriculum—that's 4,592 schools! Just over 4,000 of those schools (4,055 to be exact) chose to use it!

:: 315,813 students were reached for Christ in history classes, having viewed the JESUS Film.

:: We established a follow-up center and eventually sent out over 2,600 follow-up materials to the educators or students who had indicated that they had received Christ.

7. The financial miracle of TJTS was also huge! In all, about $500,000 was raised to see TJTS through to the end. The money came from many sources, all telling a beautiful story of the Body of Christ. Here are just a few of our financial sources:

:: Team member Scott Neel organized a garage sale to get us started. He put his heart and soul into it. He had great urgency because we wanted to get our TJTS pilot funded and off the ground in October of 1996. He raised a whopping $1,000—not near enough. The garage sale, however, was a hugely publicized event. So, as fellow missionaries learned of the need, they gave an additional $17,000 from their personal funds.

:: The Bible League gave us every Gospel of Luke we needed—over $200,000 worth.

:: Dr. Bill Bright, Founder and President of Campus Crusade for Christ, put me on the radio in the USA. As a result of his appeal, $9,000 came in at the conclusion of our interview.

:: Larry Thompson, my director, gave $30,000 from his ministry budget.

:: Donors from the USA, Singapore and Korea gave thousands of dollars, too!

TJTS spread like wildfire across Hungary! Principals jumped at the chance TJTS offered. They wanted to promote our YTL Clubs, too, because sexual diseases, pregnancies, and abortions among teens were such serious problems. During the entire campaign, 88% of all the schools in Hungary used the curriculum. Of those that used it, 95% actually showed the JESUS Film in their classrooms and 97% recommended the new curriculum to other educators and schools.

The cooperation among churches was inspiring! TJTS spread because of the belief that Jesus' message had to be proclaimed. Christian volunteers, by untold scores, went back to the schools to promote YTL Clubs. The dedication of the volunteers was amazing. One, Szabó István, a businessman, took our history curriculum and JESUS videos to 200 schools all by himself!

When you get time, check out the Appendix where you will find important information and brief quotes from volunteers that reveal the bigger picture.

The curriculum is still being taught in many public schools to this day, though the Take Jesus to School campaign ended just at the turn of the new millennium.

Shocking?

It is a great work of God that reflects His heart for the lost and the power of His Gospel at work through His praying people.

As Christians, we like to emphasize that Christianity is a personal relationship with God. It sure is. Walking with God is a very intimate experience. In the intimacy we relate to each other—God and man. We talk. Have you ever stopped to consider that our God has a voice—that He guides and directs us personally through His Word?

As we sought Him in August and September of 1996, He spoke to us through His Word in prayer. He spoke and led us into TJTS very personally.

The Word tells us that God shows the humble the way they should walk. That does not mean we will always experience something as dramatic as we did with the TJTS vision. Yet, as we look back on what happened, even while it was happening, we searched the Word and asked God to teach us. Part of the lesson He wanted us to learn was this: He has a voice and longs to teach, guide and lead us.

David wrote in Psalm 25:8-12:

"...He instructs sinners in the way. He leads the humble in justice, and He teaches the humble His way. All the paths of the Lord are loving-kindness and truth, to those who keep His covenant and His testimonies. For Your name's sake, O Lord, pardon my iniquity, for it is great. Who is the man who fears the Lord? He will instruct him in the way he should choose."

In Philippians 2:13 we learn that *"God is at work in us (in our mind, will, emotions, thoughts and plans) both to will (He works in our desires and choices) and work (to give us the capacity for doing something He wants done) for His good pleasure."* The Word says that He has gifted us for works of God.[2] *"He works in us, equipping and empowering us to do those things pleasing in His sight."*[3]

All of our working, as we work out our salvation, depends on His working in us. He gives us the capacity to do what pleases Him. He inclines our will to want what He wants, and then enables us to do it. Isaiah says, *"O Lord, you have done for us all our works."*[4]

We believe the Holy Spirit prompted us to do TJTS. He impressed upon our hearts and minds and led us in a most certain way.

What we are learning is that the leadership of God the Holy Spirit will always honor His Word. It will be accompanied by a grateful heart and holy motives. It will encourage the people of God. It will be in line with godly counsel and under an accountability relationship with your Christian leaders. The leadership promptings of others who claim to have heard from the Holy Spirit should never be trusted if the person announcing them does not clearly obey the Word of God, have an increasing knowledge of the Word of God and does not display the fruit of the Spirit in his or her life.[5]

Our God has a voice.

---

2. 1 Corinthians 12:6
3. Hebrews 13:21
4. Isaiah 26:12
5. Jack S. Deere, *Surprised by the Voice of God*, (Grand Rapids, MI: Zondervan Publishing House, 1996) adapted from 323-27.

Section Eight

:: **Beyond the Iron Curtain** ::

... Expansion

:: Expansion ::

(1997 - 2009)

He continued, "A non-Christian led her to the Lord."

"I would like to thank you for the impact that YTL had in our school. Its effect on our students' lives can barely be captured in words. Not long ago we had a ten-year class reunion for a class that graduated in 1999. As they recalled their student years, student after student mentioned that the greatest impact and their most precious hours spent in school were in the YTL interactive sessions. Because of your program we received a special award from the government that only 20 schools have ever received in the entire nation. Our success is your success.

Thank you!"

—Ferenc Móra, Primary and Art School, Répcelak, Hungary; April 27, 2009

"YTL is a beam of light in our desperate world."

—The Chief of the City Nurses Association,
Békéscsaba, Hungary; October 25, 2000

T hese are just two of the many thousands of comments we have received since YTL was launched in 1994.

We feel as though we have been walking on holy ground. A childlike joy has gripped us over these years. It feels like the paths we are on have never been traveled before. But without any question, God has been leading us on this unusual journey. Every step has presented new challenges and wonderful surprises at the same time. Each day we had no idea where God was going to lead us. Day-by-day we experienced something new—it was often surprising and always something we had never done before.

Christian volunteers call us with unbelievable stories of how God used YTL in their ministry and how they have launched youth groups in their churches. Educators are constantly sharing stories of how they were able to impact their students' lives through YTL. Students' lives are changed because of the programs and resources utilized by the creative volunteers in the YTL program.

Due to the uncontrollable and diversified nature of this movement, it is almost impossible for us to share the full extent of how God has expanded the impact of YTL. As we write in the summer months of 2009, we celebrate the 15th anniversary of the miracle of Youth at the Threshold of Life in Hungarian public schools.

In this chapter we desire to share some of the blessings we've experienced. We desire to encourage faith in the Lord Jesus Christ and glorify God for His mighty works in this ministry. With these two sentiments in mind, we humbly continue telling our story. As you read in the previous chapters, it is obvious that our own efforts and best intentions only led to frustration, doubt and failure. But every story we mention—and even every statistic—represents that God can do the impossible. He can and wants to use anyone willing to be broken before Him, available to Him, and willing to trust Him in obedience no matter what the path looks or feels like.

:: Accreditation and the Gospel ::

A key delivery strategy for YTL is to hold three-day symposiums for educators. The symposium gives us an opportunity to deliver the basic concept of YTL. During a YTL Symposium, we model and teach part of the curriculum, as well as introduce the entire curriculum. The curriculum is over 1,000 pages long and consists of three volumes and four DVDs. The curriculum contains the Gospel of Jesus in four different places, including the JESUS Film, some apologetic articles, a testimony and a copy of the *Four Spiritual Laws*—a clear presentation of the Gospel written by Dr. Bill Bright.

Let's hit the pause button right here. Would you join us in praising God? It is still very hard for us to believe that God chose us to do this. We don't fit any profile for this kind of work, including not having PhDs in education. Yet, now this curriculum and training is accredited by the Hungarian government.

The miracle of accreditation is a huge blessing, opening many doors of opportunity. In order for every educator in Hungary to remain certified to teach in public schools, they must receive 120 post-graduate credits every seven years. YTL was given the sponsorship, right and authority by the Hungarian Ministry of Education to award 30 credits to the educators who attend two symposiums and do well on their homework and writing assignments. In other words, through YTL, educators can get one-fourth of the credits needed for keeping their diploma! More profoundly, as we share the Gospel clearly at each symposium, they get those credits for hearing the Good News of Jesus Christ!

YTL Symposiums provide an excellent atmosphere in which to share the love of God. By the second night of the symposium, educators are at a point where their hearts are ready to hear something they have never heard before. Gábor shares, in a creative way, the personal journey of a little boy. This journey begins with an abusive earthly father and leads to our loving Heavenly Father. As he continues to read this tragic tale of abuse, you can hear a pin drop. All are touched. All are glued to the story. As Gábor continues to share, he reveals that this is his personal story. He then shares the Gospel in a way that touches their hearts deeply. They can identify with the story through either their own personal experience or through one of their students' experiences. The Gospel presentation is not superficial, but clear, direct and emotionally engaging.

After the Gospel presentation, we ask them to fill out a comment card. The responses on those comment cards describe the depth of impact YTL has made in the lives of the educators and their students. God is touching hearts and changing lives through the Gospel.

Here are some of those comments:

"Two years ago I heard your story. It touched me deeply! I remember that I felt I wanted to go up to you and give you a hug. I really respected you for the way you were able to share your story with us. Today, as I heard your story again, it had a much different impact. The story was, of course, not new to me, but two years ago I was far from saying that prayer. But tonight I said it! I received Christ! The story you started two years ago has now helped me to say that prayer. Thank you!"

—an educator, 2002

"It was honest and shocking. One of my students went through something similar. He wanted to commit suicide. Jesus Christ helped him to start a new life. He helped me, too."

—high school teacher, 2001

"I went through a similar situation. I couldn't forgive or forget my father and his abuse. Yet, tonight your story helped me make an important decision. In my heart I forgave him tonight. I now have peace. Thank you for helping me make that important decision."

—Tamás, 2000

:: Jesus in Public Schools ::

Over 75% of the educators who attend a YTL Symposium leave committed, not only to using the curriculum, but to showing the JESUS Film in their YTL classrooms, too.

In the past fifteen years, while with us at a weekend symposium, over 8,000 educators from twelve different nations have heard the Gospel personally through Gábor, Dave and the JESUS Film. Those attending represent a wide spectrum of educators: elementary, high school and college teachers, social workers, policemen, nuns, military chaplains, sex educators, psychiatrists, Center for Disease Control specialists, clergy and doctors and nurses who are teaching health classes in schools. These educators have been teaching YTL in Hungary to more than 383,000 students, of which over 295,000 actually saw the JESUS Film in their classrooms. How do we know this? We take extensive surveys and make annual evaluations.

The following quote is from an educator who sent us a letter. It gives a glimpse of how educators are teaching this program and how some of them who became Christians are utilizing it for sharing the Gospel in their classrooms.

> "I have been teaching the YTL program for two years in the 7th grade at Attila József Primary School in Esztergom. Both students and parents like it very much. I myself have been a Christian for eight years. I teach the entire program. I teach each lesson over a two-hour period, rather than one. This is for several reasons: children in the 6th and 7th grade are fairly young for the material and need more time to discuss and understand it. We have watched the JESUS Film together. I am now sending you the enclosed response cards with a grateful heart. There are 22 students in the class. Everyone received a Gospel of Luke last year. Some of them requested and received a new one this year because they had lost it.
>
> I also teach the program at a foster home in Párkány, Slovakia. The headmaster of the foster home asked us to help him prevent teenagers from using drugs. By teaching this program we are able to take the Gospel to our foster kids! Additionally, more and more children come out to the Bible classes that we offer in the afternoon. On behalf of the children, I give thanks to all of you for all of your work. I wish you further success in promoting and teaching the program."
>
> —Magdolna Radácsi, Esztergom. 2002

The momentum created by the YTL symposiums has opened new avenues for us to get the Gospel to many different segments of society. Educators and school principals have been constantly calling us to speak at their schools. People write to us all of the time. Sometimes they approach us on the street or at restaurants and say things like, *"I'm in your movement, too"* or *"I'm working in YTL."* In 1997 a government agency even approached us asking us to make YTL a vocation.

We often find ourselves at a place where we cannot fulfill the many requests we receive. The need for our program leads us from city to city, school to school, and symposium to symposium. Even as we write this book and look back at just the past three months, we have counted over 200 classrooms in which YTL volunteers and staff members have spoken throughout Hungary. During that short period of time, they held thirteen high school assemblies. Schools cancelled regular classes for the entire day and made it mandatory for all students to come and listen to one of the volunteers speaking on various YTL topics. The most popular sessions are entitled: *"Why Wait for Sex Until Marriage?", "Friends for Life"* and *"How to Say 'No' to Drugs."*

It continues to amaze us that after sixteen years we can walk into a school principal's office and find them more than willing to hold assemblies for every student in their school. These school assemblies provide excellent platforms for us to invite students to different YTL activities, such as YTL weekly meetings, special outreaches, YTL retreats and summer camps. These opportunities seem endless. The door is not only open to the Gospel being proclaimed in public schools, it is off its hinges!

:: *Going International* ::

While hardly able to fulfill the growing need in our own nation, God began taking YTL beyond the borders of Hungary. Soon after YTL was launched, the Vice President of Campus Crusade, Dr. Bailey Marks, Sr. visited us in 1994. Honestly, they were concerned we might be getting ourselves into something that did not fit the calling of Campus Crusade for Christ International. We did not mind the accountability at all. This open door made us cautious, especially at first.

After Bailey Marks Sr. visited one of the first YTL symposiums, it became obvious to our leadership that God had opened up something radically new here. Our Vice President wanted to take the concept and strategy of YTL worldwide and start an international ministry. He asked Dave to consider helping it get started. Dave declined so he could focus on helping the Hungarian team develop a lasting model that was field friendly.

Nevertheless, after praying about it, we decided to help. In 1995, along with a newly assembled international team, YTL was launched globally with one minor change. Originally they were using the name Youth at the Threshold of Life, but opted to change it to *"Youth at the Crossroads."* They found that the name *"Crossroads"* would communicate more meaning in an international context. Dave participated in training the Crossroads/YTL writing teams in August of 1995. Crossroads slightly changed the emphases in the program, too. It was felt that the countries they wanted to serve (mainly developing countries) would need a stronger emphasis on the topic of AIDS than we needed in Hungary.

While Campus Crusade was taking Crossroads/YTL internationally, the Hungarian YTL Team began to help neighboring countries in Eastern Europe and Russia. Ministries from various nations wanted to see if YTL could be used in their countries, curious to see if this kind of momentum could create new ministry opportunities for them. We began to hold symposiums in Hungary and invited guests from other nations to join us. During the course of our three-day YTL symposiums, many of our international guests would ask us questions about how to start YTL in their nations. As our symposiums concluded, we would invariably receive invitations to come to their countries to help them launch YTL. In 1997 YTL went to Ukraine and Romania, followed by Bulgaria a few years later.

Bulgaria, after suffering under communism for decades just like Hungary, was just a few years into her newly established democracy. In 2001 a group of military leaders from the Bulgarian Army visited our YTL Symposium in Budapest, including the Director of Military Training for Bulgarian war colleges and military academies. As we met with them during the YTL weekend, they told us of a unique problem they faced. Many of Bulgaria's young soldiers were suffering from various physical and emotional issues. These men had come to our symposium in Hungary to investigate new ideas as to how to solve this problem.

They were so touched by the symposium that they presented Dave with a special military award, the Medal of Outstanding Achievement. As they presented this medal they said the following, *"This medal is only given to soldiers who have fought on the frontline. You are fighting on the frontline to save our youth."* Dave was stunned by this honor. God was giving us favor in amazing places among influential leaders in another part of the world. Following the presentation, they extended an invitation to us. The next year we found ourselves in Sofia, Bulgaria holding a symposium for military, educational and governmental leaders. We signed a contract with them giving them the right to adapt our curriculum to teach it in the psychological departments of their war colleges.

Today, Crossroads and YTL are being taught in over 60 countries. Each country represents a special story. One of those stories remarkably highlights perhaps the most meaningful contribution YTL has ever made. In 2004 an Asian country extended us an invitation to teach YTL in the universities of its nation. Dr. Bánhegyi came with us to speak at the first YTL Symposium in the capital city of this nation. Over 140 university professors attended. That weekend we experienced déjà-vu. We felt like we were going back in time to our first symposium in Hungary. God was again cutting through "bars of iron." YTL is now widely used among university students of this country. In fact, it is taught in prominent teacher training universities in order to give diplomas certifying teachers to take YTL throughout their country.

Although for security reasons we cannot divulge specific detail, we are sure that the story God is writing on thousands of souls in this Asian country will forever bear great fruit and bring Him great glory. Surely one day in Heaven that story will be heralded describing God's amazing work. We truly consider the opportunity to launch YTL there as one of the greatest blessings of our lives.

God started YTL in the small post-communist nation of Hungary. The tools, programs and materials are now utilized in countries all over the globe. God used a small and unknown nation, a few fumbling missionaries and an honorable, compassionate, yet non-believing doctor to open many avenues for the Gospel in influential countries around the world.

This, along with every part of the YTL story, proves the truth of 1 Corinthians 1:26-29: God uses the weak, the foolish and the lowly. As a matter of fact, He will only use those who consider themselves weak, foolish and lowly. *"The Lord always starts with the small"* was Edina's Grandfather's motto, himself a persecuted Baptist pastor. The story of YTL is evidence of this truth.

:: The Tension in the Expansion ::

The growing needs and opportunities YTL generated within Hungary and in other countries came with many demands. We felt that we could not say no to these growing requests. Becoming aware of other countries' needs drove us. The opportunities obligated us. The privilege of these opportunities carried a humbling and scary responsibility. We often wondered how to keep moving forward without compromising our call to evangelize people and build disciples.

We felt that Augustine was right when he said, *"What God requires, He always provides. And what He provides, He always requires."* God provided this opportunity, but the opportunity required what we did not have. Manpower and finances were always in low supply. Yet, God has both.

The growth of YTL truly challenged our manpower. No one on the YTL team was in a position to give total focus to YTL because we always had other significant ministry responsibilities tugging at us. Yet, God decided to bless it. YTL was truly out of our control from the very beginning. That's what keeps us on our knees to this day.

Since the early years of YTL we have been aware of the uncontrollable nature of this ministry. Yet, it still feels uncomfortable. The calling and convictions God had given us drove us to make sure that personal ministries of evangelism and discipleship be developed locally. So, why was God giving us this opportunity that seemed to be taking us to the whole world? It was and is way beyond where we ever imagined we would go and much faster than we ever wanted to go. We constantly felt the tension and struggled with priorities and other responsibilities. We knew that Jesus helped the multitudes, but really spent time building into his twelve men—teaching and training them. How were we supposed to do this and maintain proper balance with our families, our quiet times with the Lord, our mission values and this global movement?

In 1998 we made a significant step toward dissolving the tension we felt. Built on the opportunities YTL generated, Dave asked Dan Butts, a veteran Crusade missionary in Budapest, to launch a direct, local Budapest High School Ministry. The impact of YTL on high schools in Budapest seemed to demand it. As we launched this new ministry, our prayer and desire was two-fold: 1) to utilize the momentum and opportunity YTL generated in the schools and build a multiplying ministry of evangelism and discipleship from the foundation and reputation of YTL, and 2) to build a high school ministry model from which churches could benefit. We wanted to provide training, encouragement and mobilization for the Body of Christ.

Dan, his wife Kelly, and their small team's wonderful job eventually gave birth to two student ministries under the umbrella of YTL. One of those ministries focused on high school students and the other on university students. YTL provided credibility, access and open doors for our staff. They were now able to freely walk into schools and onto campuses, teach in classrooms and invite students to our outreaches. Better yet, they were free to promote Christian values and share the Gospel. YTL soon became a movement among students all over the city.

Today there are YTL fan clubs on Facebook, on YouTube and on iwiw (the Hungarian version of Facebook). Each year the YTL ministries are reaching 25,000 students with the Gospel in Budapest high schools and universities directly led by these two YTL teams. Each year new generations of students are being introduced to Jesus and getting involved in discipleship groups that ground them in their faith. With this training more and more students are sharing Christ with other students. The momentum generated by the credibility of YTL was the starting point. God has opened doors to a vast harvest that has led to thousands of changed lives. Many are coming to know Him and living in glad surrender to Jesus.

Launching these student ministries was extremely important. Their success proved that YTL actually worked and was getting closer to our ultimate calling: reaching the lost and building disciple-making evangelists. These accomplishments proved that YTL is not just a social club nor is it just a fan club on Facebook. It is not just an educational program nor is it just a tool to get the Gospel to the masses. Rather, it is an excellent opportunity to get to the heart of our calling.

We felt that YTL was finally being used the way God meant it to be used. We were also beginning to see the balance between helping the masses while building into a few whom God may be calling to go further with Him. As Jesus was going to the masses, He focused on the twelve. Our "twelve" became the high school and campus movements of YTL.

The ministry model Jesus left behind makes it obvious that while He deeply built into His disciples' lives, He did not neglect the needs of the multitudes.

Mark 8 shows a clear example of how Jesus reacted to the needs of the multitude. When He saw them hungry, He fed them. As a matter of fact, He told His disciples to feed the people. Jesus was aware of where people lived and what their needs were. He always touched them personally. He touched both their felt need (hunger, illness, etc.) and their real need (sin, sheep without a shepherd, being lost, etc.). He wants to continue doing that today through His people.

The model God gave us in YTL feels the same. We minister to the multitudes, but build into the few. We give the multitudes "bread"—something they are hungry for—by teaching them. They are hungry, needy and sick in many areas of their lives. We feed, heal and love them by speaking to their felt needs. They are troubled by broken relationships, by promiscuous sex, by illicit drug use, by aimlessness in life, by not having values and by not having good friends. Jesus longs to express His love to them through His Church. He wants to touch people and meet their needs, in part, through YTL. This investment of love causes them to open their hearts so we can speak more effectively to their real need—their need for Jesus Christ.

Currently, the YTL team in Hungary includes twenty-two Hungarian and nine American full-time missionaries. Only three focus on nationwide and international expansion, traveling, curriculum production and web design. The rest of the team focuses on the purpose of reaching the lost and building disciple-making evangelists.

We started small to end small! Everything in YTL—the events, the momentum, the material production, the servicing, the training, the partnership, the traveling and the fundraising started small. We are only good stewards of YTL if everything ends small, too. That is how we feel, but what does that mean?

As YTL touches the multitudes we have the individual in mind. In other words, YTL has to serve the small—the unknown, the one student, the one educator, the one parent—those who have never heard the name of Jesus. We have to help them find a personal relationship with Him!

One of the greatest stories in the history of YTL Hungary exemplifies this principle. As with most missionaries, we have the privilege of being supported by people called by God to commit themselves to support our ministry through prayer and financial giving. We call them "Ministry Partners." Rudi is one of Gábor and Edina's first Hungarian supporters who had faithfully prayed for them and financially supported them since they came on staff in 1992.

On a typical Sunday afternoon in the fall of 1996, Rudi called Gábor and with great excitement shared an incredible story he had just witnessed that morning. He and his wife were visiting some friends for a weekend in a little town near Lake Balaton. That Sunday morning they attended their friend's small Baptist church. During the service a man was being baptized who was in his mid-forties, an age when very few Hungarians make a commitment to Jesus. This little community didn't just witness the rare baptism of a middle-aged man. What made this baptism so special was something else. As he shared his story of coming to faith in Jesus, this man shared something that touched everyone.

As he stood in the baptismal waters, he said rather bluntly and simply, *"Until recently, no one in my family believed in God. We didn't know one thing about God! But six months ago, my 14- year-old daughter led me to Christ."*

People wondered, *"How then did your daughter become a Christian if she grew up in a family that had never visited a church?"*

He continued, *"A non-Christian led her to the Lord."*

Immediately, you could hear people begin to whisper softly throughout the crowd. Rudi thought, *"That's impossible!"* This did not sound right at all!

The man didn't pay any attention to the murmuring noise and continued, *"My daughter's teacher was showing the JESUS Film to her classroom. As my daughter was watching the film, God was working in her heart. She said the prayer at the end of this film, giving her life to Christ and confessing her sin to Him."*

Rudi's dismay turned to awe-filled worship. But he still had questions. Rudi approached the man after the service to find out more. He learned that after this man's daughter prayed the prayer at the end of the JESUS Film, she asked her teacher what she was supposed to do. The teacher didn't have an answer but suggested to this 14-year-old girl that she visit the Baptist church just around the corner. That's exactly what she did. Some members of that church did a great job of follow-up, and six months later, this 14-year-old daughter led her dad to Christ.

Here is the beauty of God's work. A non-Christian educator received the JESUS Film at the YTL Symposium. She used her VCR and showed it to her entire classroom. One of the students received Jesus Christ as Lord and Savior. The neighborhood church built her up in her faith and now her entire family has been changed.

On Palm Sunday, Jesus entered Jerusalem and people spread their cloaks on the road. Because of this, the Pharisees wanted Jesus to rebuke His disciples. In Luke 19:40 Jesus' answer is stunning, *"I tell you, if they keep quiet, the stones will cry out."* Why did He refer to stones? They are dead! They have no voice. Can God still use them if He decides? Jesus says that He can!

If God can use stones to praise Him, He can use a non-Christian, a spiritually dead stone to be a vehicle for the Gospel. That is what we have concluded. God has truly strained the borders even of our theology! We had to humbly admit with worshipful hearts that God is in absolute control and can use anything or anyone to bring others to Him. The Spirit of God blows and goes wherever He decides.

:: Multiplying the Model and Mobilizing the Church ::

We have never considered YTL as ours. Nor have we ever claimed any rights or royalties. We are not the owners of this gift from God. We have always known that YTL was for the Body of Christ. We just happened to become stewards of it. We long to see more people mobilized and encouraged. Helping pastors, youth workers and layman from churches utilize this God-given tool has always been one of our focuses.

A great example of a mobilized and trained Christian volunteer is Lajos from Kecskemét, a member of the Baptist church. He started to use YTL in the school where he was a teacher. He bravely went beyond his school's border and approached the local government with some ideas. The district authorities authorized him to host a day-long symposium for every educator in his city. It went so well that the government opened and sponsored a Friday night YTL Club to compete with the discos—offering the kids a great alternative.

Gergő from Szeged is another great example of someone stepping out of his comfort zone. Gergő is a car repairman and committed Christian who wanted to reach young people in his city. After he completed the YTL Symposium and a special YTL Volunteer Training, Gergő, who is not a teacher and doesn't have a university degree, walked into the schools of his city and offered his help to give YTL talks in classrooms! Because of the good reputation of YTL, the school principal took the risk and offered a classroom to Gergő. He allowed him to teach just once. The school loved the way he taught and connected with the kids so much that he was given other opportunities. Besides regularly teaching the kids, he also started YTL clubs that meet after school. Today, Gergő trains other Christian volunteers from surrounding towns and villages how to utilize YTL and how to start local youth ministries in their churches.

:: Unusual Resources ::

As Augustine said, *"God truly provides what He requires."* On countless occasions we experienced God's supernatural provision. Every step we took challenged our faith. When YTL began we had no money. Nulla. Nada. Zip. You can imagine the hundreds of thousands of dollars it has cost over the years to reach hundreds of thousands of students in their classrooms, to publish books, to host events and to run summer camps.

Yet, during the past sixteen years there was not one time when the Lord did not provide for what He wanted done. Sometimes He provided in very unusual ways. For example, in 2004 we held a very large YTL Symposium, the largest in

YTL/Crossroads history to date. Over 800 educators came from twelve different nations to our Tenth Anniversary YTL Jubilee Symposium. You can imagine how badly we wanted to do something special for this particular symposium. We decided that we wanted to distribute our YTL curriculum at no charge to all who attended. We felt this was the Lord's leading, but we didn't have the resources to pull it off.

As we prepared and prayed for this special symposium, God gave us a bizarre idea. We sent a proposal to the Central Government of the European Union (EU). We were not sure they would even consider extending a grant to us, knowing that Christian values taught in YTL were controversial in many European circles. Something amazing happened. It was a great surprise to receive $35,000 from the EU!

That year the liberal, non-Christian European Union government out gave the Body of Christ. That year we received more support from the EU than from all of our Christian resources combined.

God truly owns all of the resources in the world. He will move everything to provide for His children as they pursue His mighty purposes.

"Not to us, not to us, but to Thy name be all the glory forever and ever! Amen!"[1]

---

1. Psalm 115:1

Section Nine

:: The Outrageous Promise ::

:: Obliged ::

"Praise the Lord! I will give thanks to the Lord with all my heart; in the company of the upright and in the assembly. Great are the works of the Lord. They are studied by all who delight in them. Splendid and majestic is His work, And His righteousness endures forever. He has made His wonders to be remembered."

—Psalm 111:1-4a

In Psalm 111 David celebrates the works of God in the company of His people. Every line in this Psalm gives praise to the Lord.

:: Remember God's Works ::

His wondrous works are *"to be remembered."* As we lift Him up *"with all of our hearts"* recalling what He has done, He overshadows the mire that often accompanies our everyday lives. When we dwell on things worthy of His praise, great things happen. Doubt, criticism, despair and self-pity give way to the majesty of God. Our hearts are renewed by the joy of knowing Him in all of His glory.

God intended for His works to remain in the memories of His people! The Hebrew people made sure they remembered key events such as God giving them the Mosaic Law or the Exodus from Egypt. Lessons God taught during their sojourn in the wilderness were constantly brought before their minds!

D. A. Carson warns us, *"One cannot long read Scripture without pondering the sad role played by forgetting. To our shame, we forget all the things we should remember."*[1]

:: Study God's Works ::

As we remember, we are to go one step further. We are to exercise our minds and study the works of the Lord. What does that mean? We are supposed to study the works of God?

Charles H. Spurgeon offers crucial insight.

> *"The hidden wisdom of God is the most marvelous part of His works, and hence, those who do not look below the surface miss the best part of what He would teach us! Because the works of God are great, they cannot be seen all at once, but must be looked into with care."* [2]

When we look back on the works God has done, we are to call them to mind carefully. We are to investigate them. Only then, as we *"strengthen our spiritual eye,"*[3] do we see the glory of God fully in His works and grow in our knowledge of Him.

Here is an example of what we mean. It is a delight for us to remember what God did in the fall of 1996. YTL was two years down the road, but Take Jesus to School (TJTS) was only an idea being tested at that time. The team faithfully went to school principals to make them the offer to teach our new Christian history supplement. After just two months of the trial we were amazed. In the first 195 schools we contacted, 179 of them accepted the offer and taught the material. That's 91%! In less than two months, 23,118 students heard the Gospel and were given a chance to receive Christ. The Gospel of Luke was given to 15,894 of them.

---

1. D. A Carson, *For the Love of God* (Wheaton, IL: Crossway Books, 1998) page for February 18.
2. Charles H. Spurgeon, *The Treasury of David*, Volume 3 (McLean, VA: MacDonald Publishing Co) page 2.
3. ibid.

We see the love and power of God in this mighty work. It shows us something beautiful and deep about the very character of God. Christianity was being embraced in a nation that had disregarded and even mocked it for 45 years! God's power was on full display as we went from school to school with TJTS. He was opening a door that He wanted the church to not only walk through, but to remove from its hinges. Very personally, as we look back and study this work of His in TJTS, we discovered two huge things: 1) God loves to use weak, average and broken people, and 2) He can do anything He wants. Nothing is impossible for Him!

Remembering and studying God's works cause us to fall deeper in love with Him and experience the joy of delighting in His glory.

:: Announce God's Works::

God's works are not only to be remembered and studied, they are to be announced! Sharing them *"in the company of the upright and in the assembly"* is important, too. Among God's family, His mighty works are to be told to one another.

For us, the works of God in YTL and TJTS are not to be remembered for an hour and then forgotten. His works are perpetual signs that share important truths about who He is. Over the years, we have been strengthened during trying times by simply remembering what God has done and praising Him together.

Consider what the Psalmist, Asaph, writes in Psalm 78:1-11.

> *"I will utter...what we have heard and known...we will not conceal them from their children, but tell to the generation to come the praises of the Lord, and His strength and His wondrous works that He has done...which He commanded our fathers that they should teach them to their children, that the generation to come might know, even the children yet to be born, that they may arise and tell them to their*

children, that they should put their confidence in God and not forget the works of God, but keep His commandments, and not be like their fathers…a generation that did not prepare its heart and whose spirit was not faithful to God. The sons of Ephraim…turned back in the day of battle. They did not keep the covenant of God and refused to walk in His law; they forgot His deeds and His miracles that He had shown them."

Asaph shares with great boldness what he had been witnessing. In this Psalm he lists miracles God did for Israel. The mighty works of God inspire him to dedicate 72 verses to honor and teach the works of God. It seems that he recites God's mighty deeds for two reasons: 1) that all may worship and glorify God and 2) teach the next generation about the nature of God.

Psalm 78 is the second longest Psalm of the 150 written and bound within the pages of our Bible. It is devoted to teaching something to every generation. God never stops working. He does things today and will tomorrow. He keeps revealing Himself in His works and teaching His truth to each and every generation. Each generation has witnessed the miraculous deeds of the Almighty. Every generation has the privilege to enjoy and benefit from the free gifts of God.

Psalm 78 and 111 teach us something about debt. God's works are like investments. These investments are for us to learn from and then teach what we learn to others. In a way, God has put each generation into debt. This debt comes with two obligations.

One debt is God-ward. We are obliged to worship God from the heart! This is not a legalistic chore because as we look back and remember what He has done, adoration for God wells up in our hearts and spills over into praise.

The other is man-ward. We are obliged to teach the next generation. Asaph warns us that if we want to see the next generation walking with God, then it is our responsibility to teach from the Word of God and from our experience in walking with God. A generation's faith partially stands on the shoulders of the teaching they have received from the generation that came before them. So, one generation is indebted to the next.

We are obliged—the two of us. Very personally, as fellow followers of Jesus and your brothers in Christ, we would like to share a few thoughts we are learning along this bizarre path.

Studying His works reveals the light of His glory. As we peer into them and lean into the One who did them, what has He wanted to teach us? What might the Lord show us through His infallible Word and His mighty works?

Let's turn our gaze to His Word.

:: The Outrageous Promise ::

When people think about Jesus the word outrageous usually does not come to mind.

Yet, His contemporaries found Him to be just that. He was constantly seeing things from an entirely different perspective. When Jesus opened His mouth, a rare and radical point of view was taught.

Centuries have passed. Over the course of time, we have lifted many of Jesus' teachings from His life and times, but the most outrageous things He said are often ignored—usually unintentionally so.

There is little doubt that following Jesus is a little outrageous. As His followers, we are required to *"deny"* ourselves. We are called to *"walk by faith and not by sight."* We are even told to *"love our enemies."* There are many commands like these given to us by Jesus.

Yet, He has given us many promises, too. Among them, one stands out. It is an outrageous promise meant for us but unfortunately is often overlooked. In fact, during our lifetime, not even a whisper of it has been heard.

The remaining chapters in our story are dedicated to amplifying the whisper of His outrageous promise.

:: Use Me? Outrageous Indeed! ::

I will do "greater works than these"? What!?

O f all the outrageous things Jesus said, there is one phrase locked away in the Gospel of John that we wish to unfetter and bring out into the open. Once this whisper is heard and believed, it will change your life completely. That is the purpose for which the promise was given—to change your life! It changed our lives entirely. It is our prayer that you will be carried by encouragement into a courageous adventure of faith that glorifies God and edifies others. Along the way, God will do something special; shock you with humble joy and delight as He uses you to change the world.

Let us take you back to our journey to provide a personal context for the rest of this book. We will get to the promise shortly.

In 1986 my wife Karen and I were working in two mission fields. We served alongside many faithful staff to help develop the campus ministry in Kansas, Missouri and Nebraska. Our team in Kansas City and the staff in our area were also given a vision for establishing new campus ministries in Hungary and throughout Eastern Europe. That vision became a personal responsibility for many staff not only to serve on campuses in mid-America but throughout Eastern Europe, too. We pursued the call of God to mobilize hundreds to do evangelism and discipleship in communist block nations. As we did, this promise took hold of our hearts. And the Lord began to call us to what, at times, seemed like an outrageous life.

Even though it is awkward to take Him at His Word on the outrageous promise, Gábor and I, along with our wives, are now asking God to glorify Himself in fulfilling this promise in and through our lives, on our teams and in the ministry to which He has called us.

We could not have imagined how great the joys of the journey would be. Since 1986, when Karen and I heard the promise for the first time, we have had the privilege of moving to and raising our family in Eastern Europe. We went with fear and trembling. Yet, His promise was sure and gave us hope to press on.

As Gábor and I have continued to walk with the One who gave us His promise, we have found that the harvest indeed is plentiful. The sweet fellowship while working together, along with excellent co-laborers, has buoyed us up time and time again to claim Jesus' outrageous promise.

Here it is. Here is Jesus' outrageous promise found in John 14:12.

> *"Truly, truly, I say to you, he who believes in Me, the works that I do, he will do also; and greater works than these he will do; because I go to the Father."*

Jesus declares His intention to use us, His children, mightily for His glory in doing *"greater works"* than those works He Himself did.

We told you it was outrageous.

Perhaps you find this as shocking as we did. This promise is so extraordinary that, as you consider living in light of it, an awkward feeling may well up in you. You may think that the most spiritual thing to do with this promise is to never claim it. A humble person could never be caught dead asking God to make this promise good in his or her life.

You may look at the promise and think, *"'Greater works than these?' What in the world does that mean? Will we do something greater than the works Jesus did while on earth?"* You may even think that this is so outrageous, so contro-versial—or at a bare minimum, so out of your depth—that it is best to leave this promise alone.

As we look at the *outrageous promise* our purpose is rather simple. We wish to do three things. First, we will unlock the meaning of this hope-giving, life-altering message. Christ's teaching in this passage ties together four other imperative essentials for our journey with Him: evangelism, faith, prayer and walking in the power of the Holy Spirit. Second, we invite you to an adventure. Together we will discover something, believe something and begin to walk in something that seems unimaginable—that God really wants to use you! Lastly, we purpose to glorify God, encouraging you to place the story we've told in this context. Our stories amplify the whisper of Jesus' profound promise and are meant to both inspire and encourage you to take His promise to heart by faith.

Before going any further, let's agree to something. As we use the word *"out-rageous"* in reference to Jesus, we do not mean to associate anything impure with it. Jesus is the Holy One of God. No evil was found in Him. He is *"very God of very God."*[4] He is holy. In Him is no darkness. Romans 1:16 says, *"For I am not ashamed of the gospel, for it is the power of God for salvation to everyone who believes, to the Jew first and also to the Greek."* Paul encouraged Timothy by say-ing, *"For God did not give us a spirit of timidity, but a spirit of power, of love and of self-discipline. So do not be ashamed to testify about our Lord, or ashamed of me his prisoner. But join with me in suffering for the gospel, by the power of God…"*[5] His Gospel is the *"power of God for salvation"* and we are not ashamed of it or of His testimony. To associate anything disgraceful or shameful with Jesus would severely miss the mark.

However, Jesus was outrageous! His words, promises and perspective on life are both upsetting and shocking. He rattles our cages, so to speak. His truth is so attractive and so different it arrests our attention. He woos us to Himself

---

4. From the Nicene Creed
5. 2 Timothy 1:7-8

by radical truth and extraordinary love. He calls us to live according to His point of view.

God wants to use you more than you can possibly imagine. Is that hard to believe? You may say to yourself, *"He can't use anyone like ME. There's so much evidence to the contrary! I try so hard and fail so miserably at so many things."*

We can relate. Gábor and I were called to work with each other. For that to happen, so many difficulties had to be faced and overcome.

Karen and I had to move to Hungary. When the day finally arrived, after 13 years of waiting, we moved to Budapest with great zeal. Yet, we were awakened from the more romantic aspects of our call rather quickly. Our first task was to learn the Hungarian language. Over the first ten months, the challenge of learning Hungarian threatened my enthusiasm for God's call, as well as my confidence. Within the first three months I faced discouragement daily. I woke up night after night in cold sweats trying to say in Hungarian, *"Hang the picture on the wall."* I couldn't. Remember? I thought I had made the biggest mistake of my life.

Our call to work together meant that Gábor had to be set free (somehow!) from his difficult and ugly past. Gábor and Edina had to endure the difficulties of working cross-culturally, becoming first-generation missionaries in their nation while working with an American mission agency. They embraced their call gladly. Yet, it brought suffering. Everything they did separated them from the heart of their culture, including sharing Christ and living for Him, raising their financial support and initiating in a passive culture.

Living in the light of this radical promise of Jesus is outrageous indeed!

:: The Call to "Greater Works" ::

He wants to do greater works through you!

It is said that Lyndon Johnson, while campaigning for the presidency of the United States back in 1963, met with a bunch of ranchers and farmers in his home state of Texas.

During his speech he said, *"I am a rancher just like you."*

One in the crowd, as he withdrew a long blade of field grass from his mouth inquisitively asked, *"Oh yeah. How big is your spread?"*

Mr. Johnson replied, *"Well, I can get up at the crack of dawn, get in my truck, and by the end of the day I still wouldn't reach the end of my property line."*

Without flinching the rancher returned with this, *"Oh yeah. I used to have me a truck like that!"*[6]

That is how we all respond to something larger than life. It is so hard to comprehend something so big, something we've never experienced, that we reinterpret what we hear to make it fit the grid of our understanding. Perhaps, as you've read this story of ours, you've wagged your head in disbelief.

We understand.

---

6. *Youth at the Threshold of Life*: Copyright (c) 1994, 1996, 2001, 2009: by Timóteus Társaság

What Jesus says in John 14:12-17 is so huge, it is usually bypassed. For most, the declaration that Jesus makes in verse 12 is so beyond our understanding and experience, it is disregarded completely. *"Me do greater works than you, Jesus? Come on!"* Even though faith is one of the Christian's core values, it feels funny to embrace this promise. It is a shocking concept. It seems extreme. Indeed, it is an outrageous promise! To claim Jesus' promise to do "greater works" would leave you feeling a little ill at ease. One might think, *"I'll just skip over this one and move on. What I don't understand can't hurt me."*

The momentary discomfort you feel quickly leaves you as you read on and head to something else that fits your experience—something you are more at home with. You might even wag and nod your head saying something to yourself like, *"Jesus, what on earth were You thinking when You said that? It must have been meant only for the Apostles."*

Is there any meaning for us in this promise?

Intrigued by this passage back in 1986, God kept pointing me back to it. It completely arrested my attention. Eventually, I began to ask God to illuminate its meaning. After study, prayer and much thought, I was led to fully embrace this promise. Soon, I found myself asking God not to allow Karen and me to die without seeing Him fulfill His outrageous promise in our lives for the sake of His glory. Finally, we adopted this truth as one of the purposes for our lives.

Let's look at it together again. Hang in there as we go forward. We need to investigate this passage thoroughly. It's important to us. We believe the works we have shared in our story of God's love beyond the Iron Curtain to be an example of the *"greater works than these"* that Jesus was talking about. It is important for another reason. We think Jesus' promise is likely one of the most overlooked jewels for Christian living and ministry.

Let's look at it again in its fuller context. In John 14:12-17, Jesus said,

> *"Truly, truly, I say to you, he who believes in Me, the works that I do, he will do also; and greater works than these he will do; because I go*

to the Father. Whatever you ask in My name, that will I do, so that the
Father may be glorified in the Son. If you ask Me anything in My name,
I will do it. If you love Me, you will keep My commandments. I will ask
the Father, and He will give you another Helper, that He may be with
you forever; that is the Spirit of truth, whom the world cannot receive,
because it does not see Him or know Him, but you know Him because
He abides with you and will be in you."

:: A Comforting Promise ::

Jesus met with His disciples on Thursday evening before His crucifixion. They celebrated the Passover together one last time. John chapter 13 through chapter 17 records what happened that evening, as well as what Jesus said to His followers. These five chapters in the Gospel of John have been called the Upper Room Discourse. In this discourse we have a treasure of teaching from the Lord. It is a precious passage cherished by Christians worldwide. The outrageous promise is found near the very beginning of Christ's discourse.

During the course of the evening Jesus said something that His disciples were not prepared for. He announced that He was going somewhere and they could not accompany Him. He said,

> *"Little children, I am with you a little while longer. You shall seek Me;*
> *and as I said to the Jews I now say to you also, 'Where I am going, you*
> *cannot come.'"[7]*

This news greatly troubled and confused the eleven. Judas Iscariot, the traitor, was no longer with them, having departed to betray the Lord.[8] The eleven were clearly grieving upon hearing this. Likely, they were deeply concerned about what would become of them. They had left their homes and families. Just after the crowning achievement of their fishing careers they dropped everything, nets and all, to follow Jesus.[9] This would be like Roberto

---

7. John 13:33
8. John 13:21-30
9. Luke 5:1-11

Carlos leaving the Brazilian World Cup Championship team right after he won the World Cup for the first time—never to return to soccer again. Jesus' disciples were so impassioned by His cause and stirred by His truth that they left everything. They had committed themselves to a revolution and were eager to magnify and serve the Messiah, their new King.

Jesus' words of His departure distressed them.

Did you see the movie *Forrest Gump*? There is one scene in that film that may help us understand what the disciples of Jesus may have felt when He announced He was leaving them. Remember Forrest's running buddies? He had started the running/jogging revolution and had many followers. All of a sudden, one day Forrest Gump resigned as their running guru. He announced, *"I'm tired. I think I'll go home now."* Then he quit. He quit everything. The running revolution's founder was hanging up his Nike's and walking away. His running cronies had a look of total confusion when he parted their company. They were lost.

A somewhat normal Thursday evening became forever abnormal when Jesus *"Gump-ed them"* saying, *"I think I'll go home now."*

Matthew Henry was right when describing what Jesus' disciples likely felt that night. He wrote,

> "As they were full of grief to think of parting with their Master, so they were full of care. What would become of them when he was gone? While he was with them, he was a support to them, *aided and encouraged them*, kept them in heart; but, if he leaves them, they will be as sheep having no shepherd, an easy prey to those who seek to run them down."[10]

Jesus continues talking and begins to allay these fears. He brings hope for the future. He assures them that they will be together in heaven.

---

10. Matthew Henry's Commentary on the Whole Bible: New Modern Edition, *(Electronic Database. Copyright (c) 1991 by Hendrickson Publishers, Inc.)* Italics are mine to help understand "he kept them in countenance."

"Do not let your heart be troubled; believe in God, believe also in Me. In My Father's house are many dwelling places; if it were not so, I would have told you; for I go to prepare a place for you. If I go and prepare a place for you, I will come again and receive you to Myself, that where I am, there you may be also."[11]

This was no doubt comforting. Yet, these men were on a mission with Christ. *"What about the here and now?"* This may have been their concern. After all, they had given themselves to something. They had paid their dues. In fact, they were barely at the beginning of something they felt was very promising. Having been challenged and called, they were committed to living for the Messiah and ushering in His Kingdom.

After speaking of a secure and happy future in heaven, Jesus promises help —a source of strength and power to continue what they started. *"I will ask the Father, and He will give you another Helper, that He may be with you forever; that is the Spirit of truth, whom the world cannot receive, because it does not see Him or know Him, but you know Him because He abides with you and will be in you. I will not leave you as orphans…"*[12] They needed the help of the Holy Spirit to continue doing what Jesus had called them to do.

But what was the call? What were they to continue to do after Jesus left them?

Earlier, the disciples were challenged to follow Christ and *"become fishers of men."*[13] What did this mean? It was common for Jesus to use everyday things to bring out a spiritual principle, to shed light upon something He wanted to emphasize. In Scripture God often makes unusual comparisons between things in order to make a very clear point. For example, when God called David to be the new King of Israel he was to *"shepherd"* God's people like he did when tending to sheep.[14] Similarly, Jesus called His men from the common task of

---

11. John 14:1-3
12. John 14:16-18
13. Matthew 4:19
14. Psalm 78:70-72

fishing to the uncommon, supernatural task of fishing for men. They were called to bring men, the souls of mankind, to Christ.

The imagery Jesus is using is simple. Jesus' disciples were knowledgeable about the process of transferring fish from one element (the sea) to another (the boat). Now they were to become experts at transferring men from the kingdom of darkness to the kingdom of God's dear Son, in whom they may find redemption from their sin.[15] *The disciples had been commissioned to do the greatest work of all, the work of leading lost, hurting and spiritually dead people to salvation.*[16]

To this they were called. To this they had committed themselves. Now the Master Fisherman had announced that the fishing mission must carry on without Him—without His physical presence, that is.

:: The Call to Greater Works ::

After comforting them with the promise of heaven, He now assures them that the mission they had committed themselves to would take a giant leap forward without His physical presence. They would later understand fully that He is very much present through the Holy Spirit.

As ridiculous as it must have sounded, Jesus promised that these fishers of men would accomplish greater works than those of the One who created those fish in the first place.

Jesus' assertion is audacious. *"The works that I have done, you will do. In fact, greater works than mine will you do."* Make no mistake. That is what He said.

And He said it to you and me.

---

15. Colossians 1:13-14
16. Ephesians 2:1-3

:: What Does "Greater Works" Mean Anyway? ::

"Put your ear down to the Bible, and hear Him bid you go and pull sinners out of the fire of sin. Put your ear down to the burdened, agonized heart of humanity, and listen to its pitiful wail for help. Go stand by the gates of hell, and hear the damned entreat you to go to their father's house and bid their brothers and sisters and servants and masters not to come there. Then look Christ in the face—whose mercy you have professed to obey—and tell Him whether you will join heart and soul and body and circumstances in the march to publish His mercy to the world."

—William Booth, founder of the Salvation Army

What on earth does Jesus mean by the word *"works"* in this passage? We have to understand this correctly. Is He talking about miracles? The Living Bible (LB) paraphrases John 14:12 in this way,

"In solemn truth I tell you, anyone believing in me shall do the same miracles I have done, and even greater ones, because I am going to be with the Father."

The New International Version of the Bible (NIV) translates it differently. It reads,

> "I tell you the truth, anyone who has faith in me will do what I have been doing. He will do even greater things than these, because I am going to the Father."

The English Standard, Revised Standard, the New American Standard, the King James and the New Kings James versions translate it differently than do the NIV and LB, and all basically say the same thing. They use the phrase "the works I do." The NIV instead uses the phrase "what I have been doing" to refer to what the other versions call the "works" of Christ.

Arriving at an understanding is important. What version is correct?

Is Jesus talking about miracles of healing when saying "the works that I do?" It is likely to have been understood by His men that way in part. Yet, if Jesus were referring primarily to miracles of healing, then in order to see the promise of "greater works" fulfilled in you and me, it would mean that we would have to display greater power than raising others from the dead. Only then could we say we have experienced Jesus fulfilling that promise. That has to be the greatest physical miracle He ever performed.

A closer study of the original word translated "works" will help us. We believe Jesus was talking about a great miracle. In fact, He was speaking of the greatest miracle of all—that of transferring people from the kingdom of darkness to light—the work of evangelism, the work of the Gospel.

Before we go any further, let's talk about two things. First, how do you feel about the word evangelism? When we use this word, we hope it brings a smile to your face, yet we suspect you may feel a bit of angst. If so, it is likely that you've seen methods that were ineffective, inappropriate, and maybe even down right offensive. If that has been your experience, we understand you may strongly react to the word evangelism. Yet, we ask that you allow us to keep using it. Evangelism means telling someone some very good news. The way you tell it, however, is very important. We believe it is best told graciously, wisely, creatively and directly. That is our aim each time we engage in evangelism.

Secondly, before moving to our study of what *"greater works"* really means, it is important to understand that we are to do evangelism in the power of the Holy Spirit. He wants to witness with power through us. In the Upper Room Discourse Jesus explains that the Holy Spirit would bear witness of Christ[17] and convince the world of sin, righteousness and judgment.[18] Jesus makes it clear. He wants us to *"bear much fruit."*[19] The Holy Spirit is the One who will produce that fruit.

Later, we will discuss the ministry of the Holy Spirit and how He wants to empower us for life and for a ministry of evangelism. But for now, it is important only to get a quick grasp of the overall context of Jesus' outrageous promise to do *"greater works."* Again, we believe that Jesus refers to the work of evangelism in this passage.

I have mentioned that a close study of the original word for "works" is vitally important. Let's turn our attention to that study.

The Apostle John uses the Greek word *'ergon'* in John 14:12. *"Truly, truly, I say to you, he who believes in Me, the works (translated from 'ergon') that I do shall he do also…"* Jesus goes on to say, *"…and greater works than these shall he do…"* Although many versions of the Bible mention *"works"* this second time, it is not in the original manuscripts. It is in italics to indicate that to us. Although the original does not use the word *"work"* (*ergon*) the second time, Jesus is obviously referring to greater works being done.

By looking at the way John uses *ergon* we can arrive at an accurate understanding of what Jesus intends for us to know. John uses the same word *ergon* in many places. Let's look at other passages in John's Gospel to denote its meaning. Remember, Jesus is promising us something very significant—the

17. John 15:26
18. John 16:7-11
19. John 15:2, 4, 8, 16

outrageous promise of John 14:12. He surely wants us to understand and embrace it.

:: John 4:34 ::

Work is first used in John 4:34. Jesus had just finished speaking to the Samaritan woman. After a long day, His disciples brought Him food and urged Him to eat. He said, *"I have food that you do not know about."*[20] Confused, the disciples wondered if someone else had fed Him. Jesus then said, *"My food is to do the will of Him who sent Me, and to accomplish His work."*

What work was He sent to do? Let's reserve our answer to the context of this passage so that we can derive the meaning of *ergon*. Evidently, Jesus was referring to a task He had just finished doing. What work did He do right before the disciples came?

He revealed who He was to the woman at the well.

The work Jesus was doing then, we could say, was the work of Him witnessing to her. In John 4:26 He said to her, *"I am He."* He was declaring to her that He was the Messiah she was waiting for.

Jesus goes on to imply three things involved in work that we classically relate to evangelism. First, the *"harvest fields are ready"* for this kind of work. Second, the sower and reaper in this work have reason to *"rejoice together."* Third, Jesus *"sends us out to reap a harvest"* from this kind of *"labor."*[21]

In John 4:34, evangelism is the work implied. That much is clear.

:: John 6:29, 30 ::

Work is also used twice in John 6:29, 30. Jesus had just finished feeding the 5,000. Later, a crowd searched diligently for Him and at last had found Him again. Perhaps, enthralled by the miracles He had wrought, they simply wanted more time around Him. They may have even been hungry. Who knows? What is important is what Jesus' conversation reveals about the word "work."

---

20. John 4:32
21. John 4:35-38

Once alone with Jesus, they asked, *"What shall we do to work the works of God?"*[22] Just so it is understood, look at this question in the original. The Greek language of this phrase looks like this: *'ergazoometha ta erga tou Theou.'* The derivative of *ergon* is seen twice. Do you see it? Look again.

Their question is straight forward. Jesus' answer will surely clarify for us what the work of God is. Jesus' answer is clear. Look at John 6:29. He said, *"This is the work of God; that you believe in Him whom He has sent."*

That is pretty straightforward. The work of God—the greatest work on earth and the best thing that can happen in life—is placing our faith and trust in Jesus Christ—turning away from our sin, confessing it, asking for forgiveness and by faith receiving it from His hand. Once done, once we believe in Jesus, we become children of God. John 1:12 states, *"To those who believe in Him, to them He gives the right to become children of God, even to them who believe in His Name."*

Seeing people put their faith in Christ requires the work of evangelism. This was the work that Paul urged Timothy to never neglect.[23] Paul says that no one will believe in Christ without hearing the words of an evangelist. That is why evangelists must be sent out.[24] In other words, the work of evangelism leads to the work of God that Jesus was talking about in John 6:29, the work of believing in Christ and being saved from sin.

Let's review. In John 4:34, evangelism is the work implied. However, in John 6:29, it is explicit.

:: *John 9:3, 4* ::

Work is used in John 9:3, 4. The disciples asked Jesus about the origin of a man's blindness. Jesus told them that the man was born blind *"in order that the works of God might be displayed in him."*[25]

---

22. John 6:28
23. 2 Timothy 4:5
24. Romans 10:15
25. John 9:1-3

The meaning of the *"work of God"* in John 9:3 is clearly a work leading to the conversion of the blind man. After being healed of his blindness, the man converted to Christ and became a disciple. Even though it cost him the social stigma of being put out of the local synagogue, the man confessed Jesus to be the Messiah.[26] He witnessed for Christ. For further study, dig deeper into John 9:20-28.

In this passage the work of God led to bringing this man to Jesus. Jesus urged his disciples to work with diligence and urgency to this end, because a time is coming when this work will come to an end.[27]

:: John 17 ::

Work is used another time in John 17. Jesus concludes His Upper Room Discourse with a prayer known as the High Priestly Prayer. Immediately after praying this prayer, He went to the Garden of Gethsemane to meet with the one who betrayed Him to His enemies. Jesus was dead within 12-15 hours of whispering "amen" to this prayer.

His prayer reveals the mission of Jesus' life on earth. In John 17:4, He says to God the Father, *"I have glorified You by completing the work you gave me to do."*

Taking a more intimate look at Jesus' prayer discloses what His work actually was: Jesus came to establish men and women in a faith-walk with God the Father.[28]

In His trial before Pilate He made his mission plain. It was a mission to bring the truth to others so as to set them free. He said, *"To this end have I been born… that I should bear witness to the truth!"*[29]

This is the work Jesus was sent to do. The work of utterly changing a person's life – making them brand new! This is a work that requires sharing the Gospel so that others can see the need to repent of their sin, place their trust in Jesus,

---

26. John 9:22
27. John 9:4
28. See John 17:4, 6, 8, 18, 21
29. John 18:37

and begin following Him with grateful hearts for the forgiveness they receive. This is the work He Himself did. This is the work He sends us to do!

:: The Work That Is No Small Thing ::

Let's look at this in another way. In one sense, if something is great, it is meant to be difficult. Conversely, if something done is a small thing, we often say, *"No sweat."* A small thing is easy. A great thing is difficult. On one occasion Jesus shows with surprising flare the contrast between a great and a small work and makes it extremely clear that forgiving people of their sin was the greatest work of all. It is recorded in Matthew 9:1-8.

In His home town, a paralytic man was brought to Jesus. Imagine the scene. Likely, crowds gathered around. A man who suffered lay before Jesus on a mat. Those who brought this man were there. Maybe their eyes pleaded with Jesus to help their friend. Religious leaders were also there. Maybe they wanted to talk about theology. Perhaps they were there to interrogate Jesus, having heard stories about Him that caused them grave concern.

All of a sudden, Jesus, whose reputation was that of a miracle worker by this time, launches out with one of the most ridiculous phrases that had ever entered the ears of the many onlookers. He turned to the paralytic and said, *"Take courage, my son, your sins are forgiven."*

Think of what the various people might have thought upon hearing this. What would you have thought? Shock would have ruled the moment for me. Stunned, my humor control program may have malfunctioned. A sanguine spasm would likely have shivered up my spine causing a release of wise crack. *"Your sins are forgiven!? Which hospital did this nutcase escape from this morning?"* Oh yeah—that's what I would have said. I would have been proud of myself had I been able to manage the miracle of self-control.

Or think of the paralytic's friends. *"Sins … forgiven? Who cares! Heal our friend!"*

Although the scribes didn't publicly blast Jesus, they privately shared their bitter concerns among themselves. *"This one blasphemes!"*

What follows is important. Jesus, maybe snickering to Himself at their petty overreactions, turns this otherwise unnoticed moment in history into something that shows off His authority. He validates exactly what He had just granted the paralytic, the forgiveness of sin.

Jesus asked the scribes, *"Which is easier…?"* Allow me to quickly paraphrase. In essence He was asking, *"Which is the smaller thing? Which takes no sweat? Which among the following two options is no problem and requires little effort?"* Let's continue, *"Which is easier, to say, 'Your sins are forgiven,' or to say, 'Rise and walk'?"* He challenged them to choose. He challenged them to declare what is a great work and what is a small work.

If given the time to answer, what do you think their answer would have been? I think they would have said something like, *"'To say?' You did say 'to say' didn't you? Well, that is easy. It is much easier 'to say,' 'Your sins are forgiven.' It's just talk. Talk is easy. Talk is cheap. If one said 'rise and walk' to this one lying here before us, His craziness would be in full view. No one can heal this boy. That is impossible. Healing is the greater, more difficult work."*

Jesus for some reason didn't let them answer His question. *"Which is easier, to say, 'Your sins are forgiven,' or to say, 'Rise and walk'?"* Instead, He went on speaking, *"But in order that you may know that the Son of Man has authority on earth to forgive sins"*—then He said to the paralytic—*"Rise, take up your bed, and go home."*[30]

And the paralytic got up and went home. He went home healed. More importantly, he went home a man whose sins had been forgiven by God.

What a great scene! I wish I could have been there. In all likelihood the scribes would have been eager to answer Jesus' question and debate the issue. The question, however, was a rhetorical one. Filled with awe at the healing, and marveling at His authority, the onlookers glorified God because of Jesus.

---

30. Matthew 9:6

What does this tell us about Christ's *work* of forgiveness?

It tells us that the greater thing is forgiveness of sin. Undoubtedly, the religious leaders and onlookers thought that the greater thing was to heal the man. After all, if mere man was to say to another, *"Your sins are forgiven,"* it would sound like the talk of a lunatic. Jesus, however, is God, and not mere man. As such, at His word, the man was healed. By this, Jesus clearly showed that He had the authority to forgive sin. He also showed that the healing was the lesser of the two works. The greater thing—the greater work—would take Jesus to the cross. His sacrificial death, both great and costly, would insure this man's forgiveness.

The much more difficult thing was to forgive. This is what He came to do. This was the great work He came to accomplish for the glory of God and good of man. He wasn't just talking about forgiveness. He literally forgave the paralytic all of his sins. This fortunate paralytic may have become the first human ever to have His sins wiped clean.

No, our Savior wasn't just talking. Jesus eventually walked His talk, didn't He? He died on the cross on Good Friday. This was the great work, the difficult work only He could accomplish. In Hungary, they do not call the day Jesus died on the cross Good Friday. They call it Great Friday. I like that. After all, it was the most historic Friday in all of history.

:: Summary ::

Let's go back to the Upper Room Discourse and summarize what we have been learning.

Jesus is talking about a work of the Gospel which requires the work of evangelism. He was envisioning His disciples for continuing the ministry He came to do. Although things would change with His departure, the works He did, they would do also. They were promised to see even *"greater works."* This was a promise that, as they went out sharing the need for forgiveness of sin and the Good News of His truth and love, they would see multitudes worldwide transferring out of the kingdom of darkness *"to the Kingdom of His beloved Son."*[31]

But what does *greater* works mean? This is simple. Since a servant is not greater than his master, as stated in John 13:16; as His ambassadors, it cannot mean we will do better *quality* evangelism than the Master Evangelist did. Clearly, it was a promise to do a greater *quantity* of evangelism. It was a promise that unimaginable numbers of people would come to Christ. The first fruits of the promise ripened and dropped from the trees when Peter first preached. They saw 3,000 people place their trust in Christ in one day.[32] Later 5,000 believed.[33]

It is vital that we take God up on His promise and be people of faith. Hosts of people from all nations are out there waiting to hear the Gospel and ready to turn with faith, if only they could hear of Him in whom they need to place their faith—Jesus.

The *outrageous promise* is a promise for spiritual awakening that we as followers of Jesus need to understand. In love with the One who first loved us, with passion for the lost He died to forgive, and with confidence in His promise, we can move out in all directions expecting greater works of evangelism.

Relax. This book is not about guilting you into evangelism. We do not intend to depress you by saying that if you are not seeing huge numbers of people trust Christ then something is wrong with you. At the same time, we do want to encourage you that God is a God of great power and wants to mightily use you.

Is that something you'd like to believe?

Experiencing God's love and wisdom in bringing the life-changing Gospel to someone through you is incredible! You can feel it. God touches. Defenses

---

31. Colossians 1:13
32. Acts 2:41
33. Acts 4:4

drop. Excuses fade. His Word gets through. The lights go on. There are smiles. Angels rejoice. And you go home singing.

The stories we've shared are meant to encourage you. They are the works of God. But the outrageous promise of Christ is conditional.

:: The Condition for "Greater Works" ::

"In the supernatural cause of the Church's mission, which rests on a supernatural covenant and is led by an omnipotent leader with all His power pledged to support it, a neglect of prayer is actually a denial that God is leading. Neglect of prayer is a willful limitation of success."

—Robert Speer

During the early years in Hungary, we experienced a profound negative from an incredible positive. Although every conversation we had with people about Christ was positive, very few people placed their trust in Christ. In February 1991, I met with a missionary colleague of mine, Dan Butts, to talk about the meaning of this dilemma. It truly troubled us that so many were interested in talking about Christ—almost everyone was eager and engaged in deep and long conversations—but precious few were becoming Christians.

Over the course of a few days, as we prayed for wisdom and pondered this issue, the Lord led us to make a firm and radical decision. We called off ministry. You read that correctly—we called normal ministry activity off. We stopped almost everything so we could focus on prayer. We felt great about that decision, too.

We wrote about this in chapter 18, *"Mark 9 and the Call to Prayer."* Remember? Our prayer emphasis became a cherished tradition back then. In the next few years we were profoundly changed by God through prayer. We had new energy, wisdom and joy in ministry. Even in the ebb and flow of ministry, in good times and bad, the Lord renewed us. There was no turning back. God had marked us by prayer.

It was then that we started to see something turn around. Within months, doors for the Gospel were being thrown wide open on campuses and in public school classrooms. People were coming to know Jesus. Lives were being changed by the hundreds. Beyond the Iron Curtain in a post-communist nation, God was at work in a new way. Jesus was doing something unique in Hungary. He was fulfilling His promise of greater works. His Church was bearing much fruit in evangelism. Like the early Church, day by day *"the Lord was adding to their numbers."*[34]

Acts 1 tells us that the early church, before experiencing the harvest in Acts 2, spent a lot of time seeking the Lord. It seems this is a condition that must be met before we can walk in the fulfillment of the *outrageous promise*.

Let's look at the outrageous promise again.

> *"Truly, truly, I say to you, he who believes in Me, the works that I do, he will do also; and greater works than these he will do; because I go to the Father. Whatever you ask in My name, that will I do, so that the Father may be glorified in the Son. If you ask Me anything in My name, I will do it."* (John 14:12-14)

Did you notice the condition of the outrageous promise? It appears that Jesus requires one thing of us as we trust Him to fulfill the promise of greater works.

We must pray!

---

34. Acts 2:47

Jesus mentions prayer twice, back-to-back in verses 13 and 14: *"to ask"* in His name and *"to ask... anything"* in His name. He says it twice for emphasis, one right after the other. When He says, *"If you ask Me..."* the second time, it is as though He is looking into their eyes with determination and saying, *"Did you hear me the first time? This is important. Ask Me!"*

Lewis Sperry Chafer, former President of Dallas Theological Seminary, once wrote, *"Prayer is said to be a cause. It is because of prayer that God promises to do! He is pleased to work through preaching; but His mighty undertakings are conditioned on prayer!"*[35]

Jesus is clearly giving us a job. We are assigned to pray! Jesus wants us to be people of prayer—*"dependent-people"* and not just *"doing-people."* For mission to succeed in fruit-bearing, prayer is essential. Why? Let's look at the context.

Before giving the outrageous promise, Philip had asked Jesus to show him and all of the disciples the Father, to which Jesus replied,

> *"Have I been so long with you, and yet you have not come to know Me, Philip? He who has seen Me has seen the Father; how can you say, 'Show us the Father'? Do you not believe that I am in the Father, and the Father is in Me? The words that I say to you I do not speak on My own initiative, but the Father abiding in Me does His works. Believe Me that I am in the Father and the Father is in Me; otherwise believe because of the works themselves." (John 14:8-11)*

Jesus was talking about works. In verse 10 Jesus says, *"...the Father abiding in Me does His works."* In verse 11 He says that they should believe in Jesus *"because of the works themselves."* Jesus is saying that the works He does are being done as He abides in the Father.

Now Jesus is telling His disciples to abide in Him through prayer so that greater works may be done through them.

---

35. Lewis Sperry Chafer, *True Evangelism; winning souls by prayer* (Grand Rapids, MI: Zondervan Publishing House, 1919) 89, 90.

But make no mistake about it. Jesus actually does the work! When we pray, He continues to work. In our humility, He gives grace and clothes us with armor.[36] In our weakness, He makes us strong.[37] As Dr. Larry Poland of MasterMedia once said, *"Prayer links the impotence of man to the OMNIPOTENCE of God!"* It's true! Prayer positions us for the powerful grace of God. It appears that God has an affinity with humility. Prayer reflects our understanding of our own weaknesses and that we are humble and dependent people.

Jesus signals something significant when He ties *"greater works"* to the upcoming event of Him leaving His disciples. In John 14:12 Jesus says *"because I go to the Father,"* you will do greater works. What does that mean? He leaves and then somehow we have the capacity to do greater works than He did?

Exactly!

Jesus' words, *"because I go,"* are the signal that identifies who actually does the greater works. It is the Spirit of God who does the work. Jesus is saying, *"Because I go to the Father, the Holy Spirit will be sent."* Only then will the Holy Spirit be sent and it is He who actually does the greater works.

Let's review. Jesus promises that we will do greater works. Then He quickly follows this *outrageous promise* with two statements that seem contradictory. He says He will do the works. He says *"I will do"* twice! Confused? Maybe you are asking, *"So, Jesus, who is doing the works, You or me?"* Clearly, He is showing us that the works we are called upon to do are done in an unequal partnership. The power for the greater works is fueled by Him. He infuses His power and life in us! We know how weak we are and demonstrate that weakness in prayer.

Something else Jesus said can be confusing, too. He said *"whatever"*[38] we ask. Does that mean we can ask for a taco and it will fall from heaven in an environmentally friendly bag? Well, no—not at all. *"Whatever"* is not a carte blanche promise having no conditions. We can't ask and pray and then tell God, *"See! You promised. Now give me a riding lawnmower."*

---

36. 1 Peter 5:5-9; Ephesians 6:10-18
37. 2 Corinthians 12:9, 10
38. John 14:13

Jesus did not say *"whatever you ask."* He said,

> *"…whatever you ask in My name, that the Father may be glorified in the Son. If you ask Me anything, in My name, I will do it. If you love Me, you will keep my commandments."*

His name is the controlling element. The Father's glory is the end game. Love for Jesus is the motivation.

Loving Jesus for His incredible grace motivates us to obey Him and live for His glory. We actually want to love Him. We are compelled to. His love captures us. His mercy humbles us. Our priorities change. We want His glory. There is joy in His presence. Obeying him *"from the heart"*[39] follows. All of these are results of Him loving us first. They are results we enjoy more than resolutions we make. We know His name. We love Him. We obey Him. We live for His glory.

When someone says to you that you can use their name, they are giving you a tremendous privilege and responsibility. That is what Jesus is doing. Jesus answers prayers that honor His name. He answers the prayers of those who want to see God the Father glorified. When you know His name and seek His glory, you know His nature. He lives in you. His Word abides in you.

This whatever-you-ask promise is not about you. It is not: *"Pray. Get. Pray. Get."* It is not a license for selfish indulgence. He is promising to answer the prayers of someone who loves and honors Him; someone who longs to magnify and please Him. In the mission of the Church, we know evangelism and discipleship, along with church-planting, are His will. The Apostle Paul prayed that God would open a door for the Word. Doors of opportunity open by means of prayer. Paul prayed that, once open, he would make the Gospel clear when he spoke.[40]

The condition for seeing greater works is prayer—intercessory prayer.

In Hungary, we began to see what it might mean to see the outrageous promise fulfilled. After years of struggle and failure in ministry—trying to break

---

39. Romans 6:17
40. Colossians 4:2-4

out of the dirge of communist oppression and wanting to take advantage of the fall of the Iron Curtain—God led us to emphasize prayer in new ways. And prayer changed our lives. We did not change anything. It wasn't our work. YTL and TJTS are works of God. We just keep admitting our needs and ask for His help. That is our part. By God's grace we are learning that prayer must saturate all we do. It comes before, during and after the work of the ministry.

How is prayer going for you? It gets tough, doesn't it? We get busy and prayer gets crowded out. Before going any further, allow us to share the single greatest lesson on intercessory prayer we've ever learned.

:: *The Two Keys of Earnest Intercessory Prayer* ::

In Luke 18, Jesus teaches about prayer and faith. He teaches what is involved in praying at all times—how to pray without losing heart or passion. Jesus uses a parable to draw out the needed truth and to help the disciples fix it in their memory.

> *"Now He was telling them a parable to show that at all times they ought to pray and not to lose heart, saying, 'In a certain city there was a judge who did not fear God and did not respect man. There was a widow in that city, and she kept coming to him, saying, 'Give me legal protection from my opponent.' For a while he was unwilling; but afterward he said to himself, 'Even though I do not fear God nor respect man, yet because this widow bothers me, I will give her legal protection, otherwise by continually coming she will wear me out.' And the Lord said, 'Hear what the unrighteous judge said; now, will not God bring about justice for His elect who cry to Him day and night, and will He delay long over them? I tell you that He will bring about justice for them quickly. However, when the Son of Man comes, will He find faith on the earth?'"[41]*

Jesus asks whether or not the Son of Man will "find faith" when He comes again. Obviously, He equates faith with the widow's persistence in boldly

---

41. Luke 18:1-8

making her request. That means Jesus is teaching that faith is asking. The widow did not claim anything. Seeking the Lord with earnest faith does not involve predicting or commanding in prayer for Him to do something for us. Prayer is asking. It is not a mechanism we use to get God to fulfill our every desire and whim. Sometimes we have been guilty of what Bob Dylan sings about in his song *When You Gonna Wake Up?*[42] He asks a penetrating question about our relationship with God: *"You think He's just an errand boy to satisfy your wandering desires? When you gonna wake up, and strengthen the things that remain?"*

Prayer is asking with a humble and passionate heart. But what causes prayers to be asked in the first place? And how does one sustain his or her energy to keep praying?

This passage gives us two keys for praying earnestly. In our early, clumsy attempts in ministry, we found that we did not possess both of these keys, and therefore we were not really praying with utter dependence. But with these two keys, we began to pray with determination!

The First Key: NEEDS BURDEN ME

Intercessory prayer requires a person who has a profound awareness of a need that is personally and intensely felt! The widow had a profound need – a need for *"legal protection."* It afflicted her greatly. She was in a deeply regrettable situation. This need burdened her to the point of action. She *"kept coming."* She was *"continually coming."* In making her request, the widow demonstrated she was helpless before the judge. She was humble, broken and needy.

Without needs deeply known, we will not pray. Perhaps this is the reason for not praying.

As we consider to whom the widow made her request, we will discover the second key to intercessory prayer.

What was the judge like? He was *"unwilling."* He *"did not respect man."* He was *"unrighteous."* He *"did not fear God."* He could not have cared less about

42. From Dylan's *Slow Train Coming* album

the woman. What caused her to go back to this wicked judge and shamelessly persist? It was a combination of her need, the first key, and one more very important thing. Jesus used an unrighteous judge to get a major point across and hands us the second key to praying earnestly.

The Second Key: ONLY HE CAN

She was convinced that the judge was the only one who could meet her need. She absolutely had no where else to turn. He was the judge. He had the job and along with that job, the authority to change her situation completely.

Jesus used the extreme image of that cruel judge to emphasize that the One we pray to is nothing like the judge. Jesus is kind and eager to hear and answer His children. Yet, like the judge, God is the ONLY ONE who can meet the need! That is the second key to intercessory prayer.

The keys to praying with a faith that earnestly persists are clear. First, we must admit that we have a need. We must personally experience and confess that we are absolutely helpless. Second, we must be humble and come to God with the conviction that ONLY HE can truly help us. We must not try to master the situations of our life with self-effort. In prayer, we *"deliberately surrender control and become incompetent."*[43]

Jesus uses an evil judge to emphasize that our hope is much stronger than the widow's. God is good! He feels a deep interest for your well-being. He will come to your aid. The judge had no interest in the widow, yet he heard her. God has a tender love for you—He will hear and save.[44]

The *outrageous promise* to do greater works than Jesus did is conditioned on this kind of praying. We even see this theme in the Old Testament.

In Joel, God told the spiritual leaders to come together in a solemn assembly to pray. He promised that, if they repent of sin and pray from humble, broken hearts, asking Him to heal and bless, then He will *"perhaps"* work. He says in

---

43. *Prayer: Finding the Heart's True Home.* Copyright (c) 1992 by Richard J. Foster. Harper Collins Publishers; 8.
44. See 1 Thessalonians 1:4; Colossians 3:12; 1 Peter 1:2 and Ephesians 1:4.

effect, *"Maybe I will leave a blessing behind."*[45] God offers the hope of His blessing to His broken and praying people. But what is the hope of His blessing? Take a look. God keeps talking.

> *"It will come about after this—**after repentance, fasting, prayer and brokenness**—that I will pour out My Spirit on all mankind ... I will pour out My Spirit in those days ... And it will come about that whoever calls on the name of the Lord will be delivered..." Joel 2:28-32*

God's heart is for people to be *"delivered."* He wants to bless in this way. God wants to bring others out of sin and be saved—rescued from sin and its penalty.

In Romans, Paul wrote, *"Whoever will call upon the name of the Lord will be saved."* Paul is quoting Joel. He is quoting the promise of Joel as he teaches what will happen when the Gospel is shared with others and why it is important to send the Church out to share the Gospel.

> *"...if you confess with your mouth Jesus as Lord, and believe in your heart that God raised Him from the dead, you will be saved; for with the heart a person believes, resulting in righteousness, and with the mouth he confesses, resulting in salvation. For the Scripture says, 'Whoever believes in Him will not be disappointed.' For there is no distinction between Jew and Greek; for the same Lord is Lord of all, abounding in riches for all who call on Him; for 'whoever will call on the name of the Lord will be saved.' How then will they call on Him in whom they have not believed? How will they believe in Him whom they have not heard? And how will they hear without a preacher? How will they preach unless they are sent? Just as it is written, 'How beautiful are the feet of those who bring Good News of good things!'"*[46]

The heart of God is clear. He wants to bless us with *"greater works"*—seeing more and more people transformed by His Gospel. Yet, this work of transforming is a supernatural partnership. It is done through praying people who walk with a certain Companion—the Holy Spirit.

---

45. Joel 1:13, 14ff, Joel 2:12-14
46. Romans 10:9-15

:: Our Companion in "Greater Works" ::

"I pray that out of his glorious riches He may strengthen you with power through His Spirit in your inner being..."

—Ephesians 3:16-17

Very early in life we experience our limits. We learn what we can and what we cannot do. We make adjustments to live within our boundaries, capacities and abilities. We learn to accept them. Later in life we become very cautious—we don't step beyond our limitations because we don't want to fail. We master managing our strengths, gifting and talents so we can live a relatively convenient life within our comfort zone. We don't like stepping into situations that take us out of it. Our comfort zone is like a protective fence around us.

When Jesus gave this outrageous promise, He was very well aware of His disciples' comfort zones. He knew well what they could and could not do. He knew their limitations. The disciples' prideful motives,[47] lack of faith[48] and hardened hearts[49] were very familiar to Jesus. He was not suffering from illusions

---

47. Luke 9:46
48. Matthew 17:20
49. Mark 6:52

about their capacity, but He still gave them the promise of greater works. That means His promise was not based on the disciples' abilities. That's encouraging! God's promises are never based on what we do or achieve. God's promises are always based on who *He* is and what *He* can do. The promise of greater works was not based on the disciples' lives at all. It was not based or dependent upon what they possessed—their background, skill or strength. It was based on something that Jesus was going to give them. His promise was based on the power and ability of the companion He was going to give them.

In the Upper Room Discourse, Jesus was constantly talking about the Holy Spirit and referred to Him as *"Helper."* Here is what He says:

1. *"And I will ask the Father, and He will give you another Helper to be with you forever."* John 14:16

2. *"But the Helper, the Holy Spirit, whom the Father will send in My name, will teach you all things and will remind you of everything I have said to you."* John 14:26

3. *"When the Helper comes, whom I will send to you from the Father, the Spirit of truth…He will testify about me."* John 15:26

4. *"…It is for your good that I am going away. Unless I go away, the Helper will not come to you; but if I go, I will send Him to you."* John 16:7

The Greek word that Jesus is using to describe this companion is 'paracletos.' Jesus uses this word four times to describe the Holy Spirit. Paracletos is translated in our Bibles as *"Helper,"*[50] *"Counselor,"*[51] *"Advocate"*[52] and *"Strengthener."*[53]

In a general sense, this word (paracletos) suggests that someone possesses the capacity to give someone else real help—strong aid. This word is also used in 1 John 2:1 for giving legal defense like an *"advocate"* does—a clear reference to Jesus as the intercessor who pleads our cause and wins our forgiveness. This word can be translated *"Counselor,"* although not in one sense; He is not a camp

50. NKJV, NAS, ESV
51. NIV
52. New Revised Standard Version
53. Amplified Version

counselor or psychologist. When *"Counselor"* is used He should be thought of as one who directs or guides. In the broader sense, when *"Comforter"* was coined in our translations, it drew from Latin words that meant to strengthen. It did not mean something to keep you warm in your bed at night.

In the most clear and biblical sense, we should understand Jesus' use of paracletos this way: the Holy Spirit is the One who undertakes all of our causes and sees us through all of our difficulties. He longs to strengthen, encourage and carry us on our journey. He longs to give us the power to live the Christian life and bear fruit through us.

Let's look at another passage about the Holy Spirit and see what we can learn about our Companion in greater works. Galatians 5:17-25:

> *"For the sinful nature desires what is contrary to the Spirit and the Spirit what is contrary to the sinful nature. They are in conflict with each other, so that you do not do what you want. But if you are led by the Spirit, you are not under law. The acts of the sinful nature are obvious: sexual immorality, impurity and debauchery; idolatry and witchcraft; hatred, discord, jealousy, fits of rage, selfish ambition, dissensions, factions and envy; drunkenness, orgies, and the like. I warn you, as I did before, that those who live like this will not inherit the kingdom of God. But the fruit of the Spirit is love, joy, peace, patience, kindness, goodness, faithfulness, gentleness and self-control. Against such things there is no law. Those who belong to Christ Jesus have crucified the sinful nature with its passions and desires. Since we live by the Spirit, let us keep in step with the Spirit."*

This passage says that the Spirit of God has desires. In verses 16 and 17 the Greek word *"epithumei"* means *"strong desires"*—that is, acute desires. Have you ever thought of Him that way? This means that the Holy Spirit has severe, sharp and intense cravings. *"He sets his desires against the flesh."* This is implied in Galatians 5:17. Desires want expression. The Holy Spirit, then, has desires ready to be expressed in and through us. Those who do not walk in the Spirit, quench the Spirit. His desires can be *quenched*.[54] We can *grieve* Him.[55]

Romans 8:5 says *"those who live in accordance with the Spirit have their minds set on what the Spirit desires."* This verse suggests that people who live by the Spirit concern themselves with the affairs of the Spirit—they are preoccupied with them. So, for those walking by the Spirit, the Spirit's ambitions will drive them. His concerns will engross them. His advice will direct them. The *"things of the Spirit"* (as this verse is translated in the New American Standard Bible)—His interests and desires—compel us as we concentrate on and give ourselves to the things of the Spirit. As we set our minds on things above, we renew our minds and take our thoughts captive to Him.

Read Galatians 5:16-18, 25 again.

> *"But I say, walk by the Spirit, and you will not carry out the desire of the flesh... But if you are led by the Spirit … If we live by the Spirit, let us also walk by the Spirit."*

Walking in the Spirit means we are led by the Spirit. If we are *"led,"* that means we are following. We are exhorted to *"walk"* or, literally in the Greek, to *"keep in step with the Spirit."* Keeping in step means that, like soldiers in the military, we are to march in rank with and through the power of the Holy Spirit. He steps and then we step—in a synchronized way.

Practically, it may help to think of keeping in step with the Spirit this way. As a little child, did you ever dance with your mom or dad? I did. I can remember listening to music and my dad taking my hands encouraging me to dance with him. He would tell me to put my feet on top of his. And as I did, his dancing feet carried me along. I danced *by my dad's power* as I kept in step with him! It was effortless. That is what *"keeping in step with the Spirit"* means. Paul is not painting a picture of you and me following along in our own strength and grunting out the Christian life. Absolutely not!

---

54. 1 Thessalonians 5:19
55. Ephesians 4:30

Life in the Spirit is both a walk with Him and a journey that He leads. If someone is leading, it means that we are yielding to them and to what they desire. He steps, we step. He longs for something and we yield to His longing. We yield in faith to His longing for holiness, love, joy, peace, etc. acknowledging His desires and will, and trusting in His power.

So then, walking by the Spirit means *we yield to His leadership and to what He desires, as we draw upon His power to live the Christian life!* What a joy it is to allow Him to live His life in and through us as we yield to Him in faith!

A young boy learning the piano once attended a concert of Poland's famous concert pianist and Prime Minister, Ignace Jan Paderewski (1919). His mother took him to encourage his progress on the piano. As he sat in the front row eyeing the beautiful Steinway, his mother talked with a friend. The boy soon slipped away. Eight o'clock came. The audience quieted down. Only then did they notice that the boy had gone on stage and was seated on the piano bench. He innocently began picking out *Twinkle, Twinkle, Little Star.* The mother gasped and immediately started to retrieve her son. But the master appeared on stage and quickly moved to the keyboard. He whispered to the boy, *"Don't quit. Keep playing."* Leaning over, Paderewski reached down with his left hand and began playing the bass part. Soon his right arm reached around the other side, encircling the child, to add a running obbligato, an indispensable part. Together, they mesmerized the crowd.

In our lives the Lord finds us unpolished and weak, surrounds us with His Spirit. He gives us His Spirit to help us and whispers in our ears, *"Don't quit. Keep playing."* As we allow Him to fulfill His work to mature and strengthen us, a work of amazing beauty is created.[56]

Perhaps you have read books or heard sermons about the Holy Spirit. Maybe your understanding of who the Holy Spirit is still alludes or confuses you. Perhaps you are not enjoying the power of the Holy Spirit. Most Christians ad-

---

56. The Paderewski story is from an old Illustration book I lost long ago. I have confirmed this story with three Polish friends who know their history.

mit to an unfortunate state of existence—struggling along, guilty and defeated in their everyday lives, not experiencing the joy and power of our Heavenly Companion, the Holy Spirit.

Allow us to share with you what it really means to walk with the Helper Jesus promised to give us. First, allow us to clarify what it does not mean. Let's go back to the observation about our comfort zones. Every leadership school teaches that anyone who wants to be productive and successful in life needs to step out of his or her comfort zone by constantly putting themselves into new and challenging situations. By doing this, you will grow. At least that is the hope.

What God offers us is much different. Walking in the power of the Holy Spirit is not a leadership exercise by which we stretch our limits and somehow produce faith and build character in our lives. The life that God offers requires us to live beyond our own strength and talent. The life lived with the *"Helper"* is not a product of human intelligence or personality training. A person living the Spirit-filled life depends completely on God—trusting Him to accomplish His purposes in and through their life.

The difference between our human effort and living the Spirit-filled life is monumental. The following diagram represents the difference.[57]

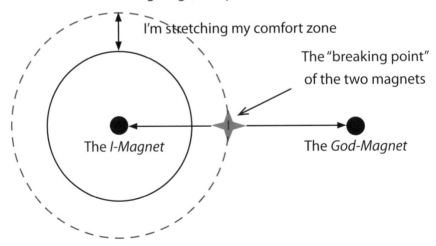

---

57. Adapted from our colleague László Baczynski, Campus Director for CCCI in Budapest

As I try to stretch my comfort zone, I am simply trying to live my life out of my own strength. The focal point in such a life is the "*I*." "*I*" live my life out of my own strength, represented by the I-Magnet. The life God offers and wants us to live is outside any possible comfort zone we can imagine. The God-Magnet is the source of that kind of life. Jesus' promise that we will do *"greater works"* (John 14:12) is a reflection of this truth.

When you put two magnets on a table and place a piece of iron between them, you will discover that the pull of the two magnets has an eventual breaking point. That point represents the place where the power of one magnet overcomes the power of the other. At the breaking point, the iron yields to the pulling force of one of the magnets.

This *pulling* happens in our life, too. The *I-Magnet* is pulling us—trying to keep us in our well- known territory. We cannot be free from self, until the *God-Magnet's* pull draws us to a breaking point. That breaking point is when we fall down in brokenness before God and admit that we cannot live our lives out of our own strength. We desperately need Him to live His supernatural life through us. The *I-Magnet* will not stop trying to pull us. The flesh is still there—in us.[58] Therefore, we do not come to this place of broken dependence only once. We come moment by moment. In order to live our lives under the pull of the *God-Magnet*, we will need to yield to the Helper—the Holy Spirit—asking Him to carry and fill us constantly.

Walking in the Spirit means we are constantly, by His grace and power, doing the following:

:: Affirming ::

We must affirm our lack of trust in ourselves. *"...They that are Christ's have crucified the flesh with its passions and evil lusts..."*[59] Paul means we are to constantly look on the flesh as God does. It is accursed and not to be trusted.

---

58. Romans 7:14-23
59. Galatians 5:24-25

Only cursed things belong on the cross. The flesh profits nothing.[60] We are not perfected by it.[61] We put no confidence in it.[62] The flesh's desires are not what we follow. Walking in the Spirit affirms that we cannot trust in our flesh and that we do not want to follow its desires. We choose humility before Christ!

Walking in the Spirit affirms one more thing: that the life we live is by faith in Christ.

As we affirm these things, the Holy Spirit is free to carry out and satisfy His desires in and through us.

Affirming includes confession. If you have sinned, then confess it. Take it seriously. It grieves God. Do not talk flippantly to the *Holy One* about sin. Our body is His temple.[63]

:: Acknowledging and Asking ::

Tell Him you can do nothing without His help. Tell God that you need *"to be strengthened with power through His Spirit in the inner man"*[64] and you want *"to be filled – directed and controlled – with the Holy Spirit."*[65] Ask Him to do what He desires through your broken will. Ask for help like a child extending his hand to his father when walking across the street in heavy traffic. *"Where do you want to go? What do you want me to know? Help me now."*

:: Appropriating ::

Appropriate the Holy Spirit's help. Anything we ask according to His will, He answers. He promises that, if we ask anything from Him that is *"according to His will, He will hear us"* and that *"we have what we have asked from Him."*[66] Choose to trust Him and His Word. We can be sure that He will come alongside to help when we ask.

---

60. John 6:63
61. Galatians 3:3
62. Philippians 3:3
63. 1 Corinthians 3:16
64. Ephesians 3:16
65. Ephesians 5:18
66. 1 John 5:13, 14

:: Putting It All Together ::

How do we put walking in the Spirit into our shoe leather? Let's get practical.

You can pray something like this, *"Lord, I'm tempted to be unkind and rash in my speech* (or, dear reader, you can talk to Him about what you feel tempted to do or say). *If I give in to this desire, I will sin against You and grieve Your Spirit within me. Without Your power I'm not going to make it. Grant me the power of the Holy Spirit in the inner man that His desires may be fully at work in me, both to will and to work for Your good pleasure. See me through this. Carry me. Empower me to 'be quick to listen, slow to speak and slow to wrath'* (dear reader, find a passage of Scripture that addresses your area of struggle). *By faith I yield to the Spirit's desire to make me patient and thank you for Your power filling me."*

Let us suggest a very revealing question that we often ask ourselves, *"If the Holy Spirit was taken from your life (or from your ministry or church), would anything change?"* What would change if the Holy Spirit was not present in your life? Anything? Is there anything in your life that could not be done by your own strength which proves God's supernatural power resides within?

Now don't feel condemned. Simply consider that you might be too influenced by the pull of your *I-Magnet.*

The life that He offers us is abundant. The life He wants to live through us is an adventure. It is different from anything we can live out in our own strength. It is only available through brokenness and by the power of the Holy Spirit.

Our Great Companion is not only helping us do greater works and bear the fruit of Christ-like character in us, but He takes us into a deeper relationship with God the Father.

As we worked together on the mission field, we discovered that God loves to knit peoples' hearts together and give them the joy of deep and lasting friendships. That is what happened to Gábor and me—two people from entirely different backgrounds experienced the power of the Holy Spirit in making us friends for life.

:: Friends for Life ::

"Two are better than one. If one falls, the other will lift up his companion. But woe to the one who falls when there is not another to lift him up."

—Ecclesiastes 4:9, 10

The more Gábor and I have worked together, the more we have learned about the power of friendship on the mission field.

The number one reason why missions fail is lack of unity on the team. Sadly, the number one reason missionaries leave the mission field is the other missionary. What a tragedy!

Jesus, in the Upper Room Discourse on the night of his betrayal, gave us a new commandment.

"A new command I give you: Love one another. As I have loved you, so you must love one another. By this all men will know that you are my disciples, if you love one another." —John 13:34-35

The love of friendship and brotherhood should dominate a team's experience. It is crucial to the mission.

The more the Church of Jesus Christ presses into the 21st century, the more common it will be to have multi-ethnic teams on the frontlines. The world has changed. It is global and you feel it, live it and experience it now, even at the local level. If people from different backgrounds can love each other as they consider the teachings of Jesus, the effect on the cultures of the world will be amazing!

The communists emphasized international brotherhood. They failed to achieve this. The words of Marx and Engels were not enough to unite the cultures of the world. They taught well. They mobilized over a third of the world within 70 years. Their philosophical message struck a cord with many. However, communism failed to produce genuine brotherhood.

When Christians unite in love, it is beautiful. Patiently, we pursue understanding each other. Diligently, we strive together for the faith of the Gospel. People take note and are drawn into the love of Jesus. It captures them and it propels us, His Church, forward.

At one symposium, a woman was captured by Jesus after seeing the love our team had for each other and for those we served. On the last day of the symposium, she stood up in front of her colleagues and said, *"I told my husband this morning on the phone that I did not want to go home. I have never felt love like this before. It feels like I am in a home that I've always longed for."* What an encouraging story for us to hear.

As I have been back in the USA, after being in Eastern Europe and serving in Budapest for 18 years, I have noticed that the Body of Jesus is struggling in the area of reaching out to others. Very few are coming to Christ. Perhaps it is due to a lack of love—lack of authentic, heart-felt, joyful love in the Body of Christ.

In some ways, it does not make sense at all that Gábor and I should get along so well. We are from two different worlds, two different backgrounds, two different languages, two different histories. We are so very different from one another.

For example, as little boys, teens and young adults…

:: Gábor never drank a Coca-Cola.
  Dave never drank a Traubisoda.

:: Gábor never sang a good hymn in a free church.
  Dave never sang the Soviet hymn in an atheistic school.

:: Gábor was never a "Boy Scout" in a local community.
  Dave wasn't a "Young Pioneer" in the Communist Party.

:: Gábor spent his Sundays doing homework for school.
  Dave spent his Sundays in Sunday school.

:: Gábor didn't catch crawdads in a creek.
  Dave never caught a whack from his dad in the face.

:: Gábor never had a Frito Chili Pie for lunch.
  Dave never had a blood sausage for breakfast.

:: Gábor never played catch with a baseball.
  Dave never said, "Checkmate" in chess.

:: Gábor relished fatty bread filled with greasy lard.
  Dave licked peanut butter from a spoon.

:: Gábor's friends were Zoli, Árpi, Endre, Egon and Dávid.
  Dave's friends were Joe, Kevin, Rick, Sam and Pat.

:: Gábor was arrested for sharing the Gospel on a beach.
  Dave was arrested for possession of marijuana in a park.

:: Gábor was not in a fraternity in college padding his resumé.
  Dave was not digging holes at a work camp building up communism.

Our backgrounds could not be more diverse. Gábor is from a broken family and a beleaguered society where atheism was honored. Dave is from a strong Christian family in the Bible-belt where God and His word were adored.

At the beginning, although we were working closely together and we both felt that God was doing something very unique, it still felt like the differences between us would only allow us to be good partners in the ministry and nothing more. We could not possibly become really good friends. It felt too hard to build a friendship between two people from such diverse cultures and upbringings. Building a close friendship would involve enormous risk, an openness to learn, and a willingness to change things that stem from deep places in our culture—things rooted deep down within our souls.

No—we'd never be friends.

Some painful experiences in the past made Gábor skeptical about the possibility of building a lasting friendship with an American. We had been working closely together for a year in YTL when, after a busy and demanding day, Gábor felt compelled to clearly verbalize his doubts about the quality and future of our relationship. *"Dave, I really like working with you, but I'm afraid I can't be a really close friend with an American. The way Americans think about friendship is so different. Friendship for me is a life-long commitment! When Americans leave, they leave behind their friends and forget them."* This came from out of nowhere for me. I really didn't know how to take this.

It was clear that the cultural, family, social and personality differences could have built major walls between us. We had different assumptions, different perspectives and different expectations. Even the same words had different meaning to us. Words like friendship.

It did not make sense to try working on a friendship that would not last. Couldn't we just be partners in mission? Did we have to be really good friends? Surely, we could just express respect and love to each other as teammates—good ministry partners! Wouldn't that be good enough?

Yes, of course, we could have. But we didn't want to. We would have missed out on a wonderful gift from God—a gift worth taking risks for; a gift worth unlearning things that had shaped our lives and personalities; a gift that was designed by God to protect and help us; a gift that breathes life into living. That gift is one of committed friendship.

Solomon said, *"Two are better than one. If one falls, the other will lift up his companion. But woe to the one who falls when there is not another to lift him up."*[67]

Life was not meant to be lived alone. Friends are listeners. Friends are care-givers and lovers of the soul. Friends are participants in life. They are promise keepers and commitment makers. They are there—loyal and true. They are not afraid to let each other know that the other has needs and fears or has experienced failure and disappointment.

Cicero, the great Roman statesman and philosopher, was right when he said, *"Friendship improves happiness and abates misery, by the doubling of our joy and the dividing of our grief."*[68]

The two key factors that keep a friendship glued together are sharing and accepting. People who do these two things will have friends. People who are not sharing and not doing things with others, for whatever reason, do not have friends. Pride, insecurity, selfishness, fear—all or any combination—prevent them from having good, lasting friendships. People can be friendly and polite, but if they do not accept others, it really shows, and it is deadening to friendship.

Our friendship grew out of mere companionship. Over time, through conversations and shared experiences, we discovered that we had many things in common—common insights, interests and tastes. C. S. Lewis says that friendship begins when that discovery takes place—when two people, to their surprise, discover that they share things in common. Then, in the sharing of them with each other, something happens! The opening of a new and powerful friendship expresses itself for the first time, *"What? You too? I thought I was the only one!"*[69]

---

67. Ecclesiastes 4:9, 10
68. Marcus Tullius Cicero; worldwide web.litera.co.uk
69. Adapted from *The Inspirational Writings of C. S. Lewis* Copyright (c) 1994; Book Three - *The Four Loves* Copyright (c) 1960 by Helen Joy Lewis. Inspirational Press: New York, NY; 255

God wants us to have friends as we follow His call. Our community around the God-given common cause of Christ forged our relationship into a committed friendship.

How did we overcome the diversities between us? It was very easy. It was simple commitment. We discovered each other's commitment again and again as we continually walked through life together and accepted each other along the path God had put us on.

The ministry is full of many uplifting moments, yet we have our share of challenges, too. Satan has tried to destroy many things along the way. Spiritual attacks are regular occurrences when you commit to God's work. While experiencing God's unimaginable blessing, we have also experienced great attacks in many areas of life, including health, finances, family, housing, ministry, church, etc. There were many times when one felt discouraged and the other had to lift him up. When one didn't know which direction to go, the other gave advice. When one was hurting, the other encouraged. Nothing anchored our friendship more than going through trials together.

In our friendship we experienced growing freedom. We can now share anything with each other without being afraid of being judged by the other or losing the confidences meant to be known only by the other. It involves huge risks—the risk to open up and hope that one will accept the other—believing a true friend will stay committed even when one is at his worst.

Our commitment to this lasting friendship did not change when God called Dave and his family to move back to the United States to serve Him there. Sure, at first, there was grief over losing the daily connection of working together, but we had no doubts that we would maintain close fellowship. Our commitment to each other has never waned.

That two families from such diverse backgrounds became friends has been a great gift from God! Even with a great ocean that separates us now, we remain totally committed to each other as the closest of friends.

We grew up in two very different cultures on two different continents under two different political systems. But for a significant moment in history, God brought us together to make a lasting impact for His Kingdom and to bless us with a lasting friendship. That gift continues to this day.

It's outrageous all right.

But there is one final question we have to face.

:: Can God Really Use Me? ::

"The world has yet to see what God can do through the man
who is totally yielded to Him. By the grace of God,
I will be that man."

—Henry Varley to D. L. Moody

Our enemy is effective.

The thought of being used by God to impact the world around us, at times, borders on the ridiculous. Satan has so bound the army of God that the thought of being strong enough, mature enough and secure enough to be used by God seems absurd. Our personal struggles have, perhaps, replaced any thought that God may want to use us to bring healing and positive change to our hurting world.

"Change the world? I can't. I am weak. I will not endure the second
step, so why take the first one? Heal a broken world? Me? I'd love to
believe that, but the enemy strongholds are too formidable."

Together, during the course of this book, we have considered things of great encouragement. We've reflected on God's works. We've looked deeply at

His Word. Now, at the end of our journey with you, we want to encourage your faith and remind you of God's great faithfulness and awesome power.

Our faith has been challenged again and again as we have faced what felt like impossible odds. We have had to adjust to new cultures, figure out new ministry paradigms, make tough decisions affecting many people's lives, deal with aggravating health issues—endure challenges of all kinds—while trying to be good family men and maintain some kind of balance in life.

Let's be reminded that, no matter how it feels or what the circumstances are, God wants to express Himself through us mightily to change the world! He really does!

If you were on God's playground and He was choosing sides, would He choose you?

Just reading the above question may lead you to a place of insecurity. You may be bombarded with negative thoughts like these.

> *"Would God choose me? Surely not! He cannot use anyone like ME! There's so much evidence to the contrary! I try so hard and fail so miserably at so many things. My tongue trips me up. I'm shy. I'm fearful. I'm not smart. I'm not a people person. I don't have any precious skills or talents. I'm average. I don't like being average."*

I remember back in grade school how tense things got when sides were chosen to play baseball. Some kids boldly shouted, *"Pick me! Pick me!"* Other kids seemed to shrink back in fear. Self-consciousness filled the atmosphere for a few tense minutes.

Were you ever chosen last? It's a bad feeling. If not, do you remember how bad you felt that a first, second, third and last choice had to be made? There was no way avoiding making someone feel small, insignificant or somehow less valuable than those chosen before they were.

Think about the high stakes involved in the heavenly realm. Who God chooses in the battle for people's souls has to be one of the biggest decisions

He makes. After all, the fight of faith is against a formidable enemy, so His team has to be made up of qualified people to win it.

So, who does God choose anyway?

It appears that His value system is different than ours. What is important to Him is important to no one else. Never forget that! We serve a God whose power knows no end and who chooses to work absolutely contrary to the ways you and I may think are proper.

Three feelings have often dominated me. I often feel weak, foolish and average—like I am nothing special. Have you ever felt that way? If so, you are exactly the kind of person God is looking for! Is that difficult to believe? Take a look at this.

> "For consider your calling, brethren, that there were not many wise according to the flesh, not many mighty, not many noble *(human standards and values)*; but God has chosen the foolish things of the world to shame the wise, and God has chosen the weak things of the world to shame the things which are strong, and the base things of the world and the despised God has chosen, the things that are not, so that He may nullify the things that are, so that no man may boast before God. But by His doing you are in Christ Jesus, who became to us wisdom from God, and righteousness and sanctification, and redemption, so that, just as it is written, 'LET HIM WHO BOASTS, BOAST IN THE LORD.'"[70]

Did you notice who God chooses? He uses the word *"chosen"* three times to make sure we do not miss it. He chooses the foolish, the weak and the base, or the average. This means that you likely qualify to be used by God to reflect His glory to the world. Notice the thrust of the passage. Paul is talking about being used by God to influence others toward faith in Him. He is basically saying that God has a very strong affinity with those who know they are nothing apart from Christ.

---

70. 1 Corinthians 1:26-31 NASB (italics mine)

Humility attracts His attention.

Paul is reminding the Corinthians that he was sent to preach the Gospel in such a way that three things were evident in the way he conducted himself in the ministry:

:: The cross of Christ is not negated in any way.[71]

:: The ministry was a demonstration of the Holy Spirit and power.[72]

:: God does it all and man is simply a bond servant in the hands of God. Man has no reason to boast whatsoever.[73]

Paul is talking about being chosen and used by God for His glory and for the building up of others. That is the context.

This means something profoundly surprising. God wants to use you. Imagine that! To demonstrate His infinite wisdom and reveal the mystery of the ages—to share the message of Christ crucified and the liberating truth that He is our righteousness, sanctification and redemption[74]—He chooses the foolish, the weak and the average. He chooses people like you and me.

Once chosen, what is the source of power to accomplish anything that would actually change the world?

In another passage, Ephesians 3, the Apostle Paul again reflects upon the wisdom of God and the revelation of His mystery. It seems that these two themes cannot be divorced from Paul's thinking about his ministry of *"preaching the Gospel to the Gentiles."* God's wisdom is *"not of this age"* (not of this world). His way of doing things is made known through His Church, His chosen ones. The mystery of His Gospel, which was once hidden, is now what we bring to light.[75]

As Paul thinks about the stewardship of God's grace given to him to take the Gospel to the world, he lifts up a prayer to God on behalf of the Ephesians. As he closes his prayer, an unusual thing happens.

---

71. 1 Corinthians 1:13-17
72. 1 Corinthians 2: 1-5
73. 1 Corinthians 1:30, 31; 1 Corinthians 3:6-9
74. 1 Corinthians 1:23-2:5
75. Compare 1 Corinthians 2:1-7 with Ephesians 3:9ff

It is typical for us to close our prayers with something like, *"In Jesus' name, amen."* We declare that we come to God on the basis of Jesus' merits, love and grace. As we make this simple declaration, we are in essence focusing on Him. It is so common for us to end our prayers in this way that we often overlook that God—the One to whom we pray—is all-powerful.

I imagine that Paul, when he begins to write the phrase beginning in Ephesians 3:20, pauses for a minute. As he locks onto the nature of the One to whom he has been praying he gets caught up a bit. You can see it. You can feel it. Paul is overwhelmed by the nature of God. Like we do so often, he is closing his prayer. But unlike us, he seems to get carried away in his reflection on God. His mind is focused. He fastens upon God and finds it difficult to describe Him. He gets carried away in a run-on sentence.

But what a sentence!

He begins to try to end his prayer with, *"Now to Him…"* In our vernacular it would be, *"In Jesus' name…"* Yet, as Paul thinks of God this time, as he prays, he tries to describe His awesome power and cannot. In the original language he uses five words to wrap himself around the description of God's might. What Paul finally writes is one of the most profound and compelling images of God in the Bible.

Allow me to project just a bit. As Paul writes his prayer, his thoughts could have been something like this (represented in the parentheses below):

"Now to Him…" (Paul thinks, "Let's see, what is God really like? His grace to me has been an enabling force to keep me strong and persevering.")

"Now to Him, who is able. Amen." ("No. That is not quite enough.")

"Now to Him, who is able to do mighty things. Amen." ("That doesn't hit the mark either.")

"Now to Him, who is able to do exceedingly…" ("Not enough.")

"…exceedingly abundantly." ("I'm getting closer, but this still doesn't cover it. No…")

"…exceedingly abundantly beyond." ("Beyond what?")

"… all!" ("Not some of. Not most of! That's it!")

"Now to Him, who is able to do exceedingly abundantly beyond all that we ask of Him. Amen." ("Wait a minute. His power and abundant resources are way beyond what I know.")

"Now to Him, who is able to do exceedingly abundantly beyond all that we ask or think." ("Hallelujah. Praise You, Lord.")

"Now to Him, who is able to do exceedingly abundantly beyond all that we ask or think, according to the power that works in us, to Him be the glory in the Church and in Christ Jesus to all generations forever and ever. Amen."[76]

Finally, Paul finishes his thought, raises his voice, rings out a song to echo throughout eternity and then, rests his pen.

Wow! What hope stirs within us as we focus on the power of God!

God definitely wants to use you and work through you—for His glory. And what a joy it is to watch Him work!

The adventure He has for you is so incredible that you cannot even imagine it. God has the power to fulfill His outrageous promise to do great works through you. In fact, His power is made perfect in and through our weakness, as we look to His grace as our sufficiency and live by faith in His faithfulness.

God has chosen the weak, the foolish and the average. Respond to His call. Believe His promises. Then, get ready. His paths marked out for you are like no other. The journey is awesome.

In fact, it's outrageous.

---

76. Ephesians 3:20

:: **Appendix** ::

What is Youth at the Threshold of Life (YTL)?

YTL is a social-science curriculum aimed at youth ages 13-16. It focuses on character and friendship development, as well as drug and sexually transmitted disease prevention. Hungarian public schools in 899 cities, villages and townships are actively using YTL programs and teaching the curriculum.

YTL is an accredited educational program of Timóteus Társaság (Campus Crusade for Christ Hungary), and is sponsored by the Ministry of Education (Hungarian Parliament), the National AIDS Coordinator of Hungary and Hungary's National Institute for Health Promotion (NEVI). The YTL curriculum is government-approved for public schools. Accredited by the Ministry of Education, YTL grants 30 post-graduate credits toward the educators' ongoing education requirements.

YTL is a nationwide teacher's training and support network committed to enhancing the professional and personal development of all educators working with youth—including public school, military, religious, clinical and medical educators.

YTL has multi-faceted programs that contribute to the lives of middle and high school students, university students, educators and other professionals working directly with students. We seek to care for and resource them in ways that help them grow personally and professionally—helping them to balance all dimensions of life while emphasizing the spiritual area. These programs include SpeakOut English Camps, YTL High School Ministry, YTL Campus Ministry, Change-Agent Peer Educators Network, YTL Parenting Your Adolescent Training, and the Story of the Soul Experience, an interactive coffeehouse for university students.

YTL has an international partnership with Youth at the Crossroads, which began in the fall of 1995 with the help of YTL staff and the National Institute for Health Promotion in Hungary. As of 2010, YTL and Crossroads are in 62 countries.

David M. Robinson (former National Director of Timóteus Társaság) and *Gábor Grész* (current National Director of Timóteus Társaság) began Youth at the Threshold of Life in 1994 at the invitation of the National AIDS Committee and National Institute for Health Promotion. Both are agencies within the Hungarian Parliament. Production of the curriculum began in February. The first edition was published in November of that year. A team of sterling staff soon formed, including Eva Mergl, who contributed to the editing process and interactive game creation for the curriculum.

:: THE GOALS OF YTL ::

1: Increase students' emotional development and help build their self-esteem, self-confidence and communication skills so as to positively affect their capacity to make friends.

2: Decrease sexual promiscuity, STDs, teen-age pregnancies and AIDS.

3: Increase understanding of the dangers of drugs and decrease drug abuse and first time drug usage.

4: Prepare youth for adulthood, marriage and family by helping to strengthen their moral foundations, value system and character development.

#5: Open doors of evangelism for ministry development among leaders in government, education and among university and high school students worldwide.

:: KEY YTL DATA (through the spring of 2010) ::

:: 5,636 Hungarian educators and professionals (i.e. medical personnel, police, military educators, psychologists, youth workers, etc.) are trained and teaching YTL in Hungary.

:: 72.3% of all trained educators show the Jesus DVD in public classrooms.

:: 411,260 students have attended our YTL classrooms; 295,320 of them have been exposed to the Gospel as participants in YTL classrooms, clubs and summer camps.

:: Approximately 1,000 active volunteers from over fifty ministries and churches in Hungary are leading various youth ministries of evangelism and discipleship.

:: ASK US AT WWW.OUTRAGEOUSPROMISE.COM ABOUT... ::

:: open doors and changed lives among students, educators, parents and community leaders

:: our tools and integrated movement building strategies

:: university students being mobilized as peer educators

:: volunteers mobilized and taking the Gospel to the ends of the earth

:: what is going on in the vast harvest of the world via YTL

:: MILESTONES ::

January 1994 ➤ Dr. Dénes Bánhegyi, National AIDS Coordinator, asks Timóteus Társaság (TT's Dave Robinson and Gábor Grész) to develop a relationship-character development, AIDS and drug-prevention program for Hungarian youth. Youth at the Threshold of Life is born.

March 24-26, 1994 ➤ TT organizes a trial YTL Symposium, attended by 150 government officials in education and health fields.

November 1994 ➤ The first edition of YTL Teacher's Handbook is published. YTL is featured on national television and at the AIDS Benefit in the Budapest Castle.

February 26 - March 5, 1995 ➤ Josh McDowell comes to help us gain credibility and momentum with both educators and politicians, as well as to reach out to university students. Josh not only spoke to thousands at various outreaches, but blessed the Body of Christ by helping us host a prayer conference for pastors and Christian leaders in Budapest. Josh also coached Crusade staff regarding how to think about the opportunity that was unfolding for us with YTL.

Summer 1995 ➢ YTL becomes an international strategy for Campus Crusade for Christ International, later changing the name to Youth at the Crossroads.

Spring 1996 ➢ YTL volunteer training begins on how to use YTL in school classrooms and in an after-school club format.

March 1999 ➢ The first YTL Parenting Symposium; 420 attend.

Summer 1999 ➢ YTL Hungary sends missionaries Csaba and Virág Balkus to Albania. YTL High School Ministry begins in Tirana.

Fall 1999 ➢ TT High School Ministry begins through the open doors of YTL.

March 3-5, 2000 ➢ The 12th YTL Symposium hosts 795 participants, including representatives from 12 countries. Many expressed an interest in translating the manual into their own languages.

Spring 2000 ➢ The third edition of the YTL Teacher's Handbook is completed. YTL and Crossroads are taught in 32 nations.

Fall 2000 ➢ The Community Ministry restarts with a primary focus on ministry to parents.

October 25, 2000 ➢ Upon the request of the Békés County Health Department (ÁNTSZ), the first one-day symposium is held in Békéscsaba. Jávor Ferenc leads this vital part of our national strategy.

March 9-11, 2001 ➢ The 14th YTL Symposium is held. By this time, approximately 4,000 educators representing 500 schools are participating in YTL.

March 22, 2001 ➢ The government officially accredits YTL as a continuing education course.

Spring 2002 ➤ YTL is used in the Bulgarian Military Academy's Psychological Care division.

Spring 2003 ➤ The European Union officially supports YTL with a grant.

Spring 2006 ➤ YTL and Crossroads are taught in 56 nations.

Spring 2006 ➤ YTL introduces new curriculum—Story of the Soul; an interactive coffeehouse experience

January 2007 ➤ The government officially reaccredits YTL.

March 2007 ➤ Through the 20th YTL Symposium 6,390 new YTL students were added to our classrooms in Hungary. Also, YTL expands to Kazakhstan and Kabardino-Balkaria, Russia.

October 2009 ➤ YTL celebrates its 15th anniversary with a new training symposium and introduces its third volume of the Teacher's Handbook. Together, Crossroads and YTL are in 62 countries from Honduras to Ukraine, from the Philippines to Hong Kong, from Malawi to Spain.

The YTL curriculum contains a three-volume *YTL Teacher's Handbook* (54 interactive classroom sessions, 14 readings, games, tests, skits and discovery tools) six videos, one DVD and three student textbooks (by Josh McDowell: *Why Wait?* and *Am I Who Others Say I Am?* and Max Lucado: *You Are Special* with a Gospel presentation by Dave Robinson, his then 13-year-old daughter, Katie, and friend Dan LaGue).

Pictures of the YTL curricula and videos

We Glory in God's Wisdom: a Youth at the

Threshold of Life special story:

I had to communicate a concern to Dr. Bánhegyi and NEVI at the very beginning of our partnership.

The more we stepped into this relationship, the more we saw how non-believers thought and the more we witnessed what they truly valued. "Waiting until marriage to have sex" was clearly not their value. It was ours. The National Institute for Health Promotion in Hungary (NEVI) had other programs. They passed out condoms every chance they got.

We were worried.

As we proceeded into the spring of 1994, before our "Trial YTL Symposium" from March 24-26, I lost sleep thinking about telling NEVI how we could not have our logo alongside theirs on our curriculum publications without a disclaimer. It would have been negligent of us. It would have been wrong. It would have offended the Church that we love and serve. It may have brought dishonor to Jesus in some way. Loosing our face through compromise was not worth keeping our partnership with NEVI and this wonderful opportunity they were offering us.

Our faith was being tested, yet God gave us grace and wisdom to see it through.

After much prayer and discussing it with Paul, Gábor and Éva, I took the following to Dr. Bánhegyi and he agreed without any hesitation to put the following in our printed material (where it stands to this day).

> "Timóteus Társaság is cooperating in the development and promotion
> of a family health education program. The aim of this program is
> to help youth in the areas of self-image, family life, preparation for
> marriage and developing moral standards as a basis for their sexual

behavior. This program is based on biblical principles, belief in God, and the importance of waiting to have sex until marriage (the meaning behind "abstinence") and monogamy. Our cooperation with NEVI should not be understood that Timóteus Társaság agrees with any other sex education or sex-health promotion program sponsored by NEVI. While appreciating NEVI's tolerance to accept other approaches to the current crisis affecting youth today, we accept the approach promoted in "Youth at the Threshold of Life" (YTL) exclusively or similar programs that share the foundational teachings of YTL."

Take Jesus to School: quotes from teachers, principals and Christian volunteers [1]

"I used it in my first grade (freshman) history classes and fourth grade (senior) social environment classes, which covers the major world religions, too. I spent five class periods with your material in both grades. We watched the whole video, too. I want to say thank you on behalf of the school and student body." (a high school teacher's comments)

"We've reached all 17 high schools in our city. At one of them an atheist teacher planned to spend four class periods on this topic. He invited us, too, to talk with the kids about our faith. We were allowed to sing and share the Gospel with them! The four hours weren't even enough—they wanted more!" (as told by one Christian TJTS volunteer from Debrecen)

"From our school four teachers took part in the training, two believers and two non-believers. That is, until the third day of the training! PTL! My beloved colleagues received Christ Sunday morning! Please organize more events like this!" (This comment comes from a Christian volunteer in Baja regarding a training conference intended only for Christians.)

"Some teachers changed their normal plans, and though they had previously taught this time period of history (The Roman Empire, etc.), they went back to show the video."

"At quite a few schools it is being used not only in history and literature classes, but also in home room, philosophy and social science classes as well!" (from the March 27, 1997 TJTS Evaluative Report)

"As we talked it went real well. Then the teacher jokingly asked, 'Could your group give our school two free microscopes?'" (volunteer from Csabdi)

"This curriculum is very carefully designed—high quality!" (Five different history teachers from Debrecen made this exact same comment.)

---

1. Any reference to "video" refers to the JESUS Film.

"They hesitated to consider using it at first. But it helped when they took the video home and watched it with their families! They liked it a lot." (from a volunteer from Boldva)

"Before I went to the school, I prayed for the principal with my mom. God answered! We had a great conversation (as I presented the curriculum offer). I even shared my faith with him. It was good to see a strict, hard man open his heart and begin to ask questions! I hope to have other opportunities to talk with him." (from a volunteer in Babolna)

"The teacher wants to use it in six class periods. She plans to show the video in 15-minute parts, and then discuss it with them." (from a volunteer in Budapest)

"They highly valued that our program was not tied to a certain church, otherwise, the teacher said she surely would not have used the closing of the video." (from a volunteer from Orgovány)

"They asked me to leave the package there for a week, so that they could make a decision. During that week, as they deliberated, every single teacher saw the JESUS Film!" (a volunteer's comments from Újkígyos)

"After the presentation I had a chance to share my personal testimony with the teacher. It was good that at FÉKÖK (the Hungarian acronym for Youth at the Threshold of Life Volunteer Training) I got training about this as well." (from a volunteer from Bicske)

"I would like to make this material obligatory for all the 1,100 students and all the teachers in my school!" (from a high school principal in Nagykanizsa)

"We wish you came earlier!" (from the Board of Educators in Nagykanizsa, Hungary)

"Why is it that Catholics never find out about these kind of things?" (asked by a parochial school principal in Pécel)

Pictures from the History of YTL

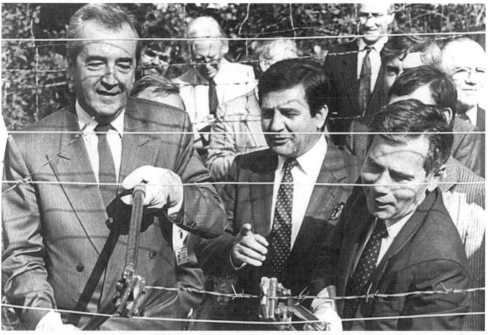

Cutting the Iron Curtain: Hungarian Foreign Minister Gyula Horn and his Austrian counterpart Alois Mock work together to dismantle part of the 'Iron Curtain' between Austria and Hungary in June 1989. *Photo courtesy of http://thevieweast.files.wordpress.com*

Left: Communist Star at Adam Clark Square in Budapest

Above: Hungarian Communist Seal

The three couples who started YTL (from left to right): Dave and Karen Robinson, Drs. Dénes and Annamária Bánhegyi, Gábor and Edina Grész. See "The Birth of YTL" chapter.

The initial trial YTL Symposium sponsored by NEVI in March 1994. Guest speaker: Dick Day. See "A Bizarre Path" chapter.

The first YTL Educator's Symposium in December 1994. Budapest, Hotel Regina. See "YTL's First Symposium" and "The Klára Profile" chapters.

Dave speaking at the second YTL Symposium while Edina is translating for him in November 1995. Budapest, Hotel Regina.

Dave was the only foreigner who addressed the attendees at the National AIDS Convention in November 1994. See "The AIDS Convention" chapter.

YTL Symposium in the former Headquarters for the Budapest Communist Party in November 1997. This is where Éva stood up in front of 450 colleuges. See the "Irony" chapter.

YTL Symposium in 1999 at the Karl Marx Economic University, a former communist training center.

Dave and Gábor speaking at the Tenth Anniversary YTL Jubilee Symposium in 2004 to over 800 educators in 2004. See the "Expansion" chapter.

A group of newly accredited educators approved by the government to teach YTL in their public classrooms. See the "Expansion" chapter.

Bulgarian National Television interviewing Dave and Gábor after the YTL Symposium in Sofia, Bulgaria. See the "Expansion" chapter.

Training over 1,000 Christian volunteers who will "Take Jesus to School" from 1996-1999. This mobilization led to hundreds of thousands of students viewing the JESUS Film in their public schools. See the "Take Jesus to School" chapter.

Dave speaking at the Fifteenth Anniversary YTL Jubilee Symposium in Budapest in 2009. See the "What is Youth at the Threshold of Life?" chapter in the Appendix.

A YTL high school assembly; schools are canceling classes to gather their students in the school's gym to listen to our staff teach various YTL sessions.

Students in a YTL class; educators are leading YTL classroom discussions in hundreds of schools each year.

Maps of Eastern Europe and Russia in 1989 and 2010

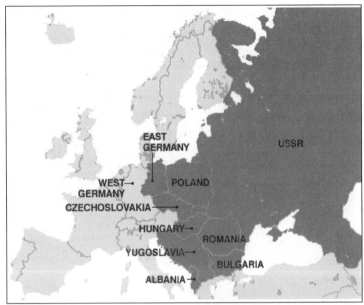

Maps of Hungary 2010

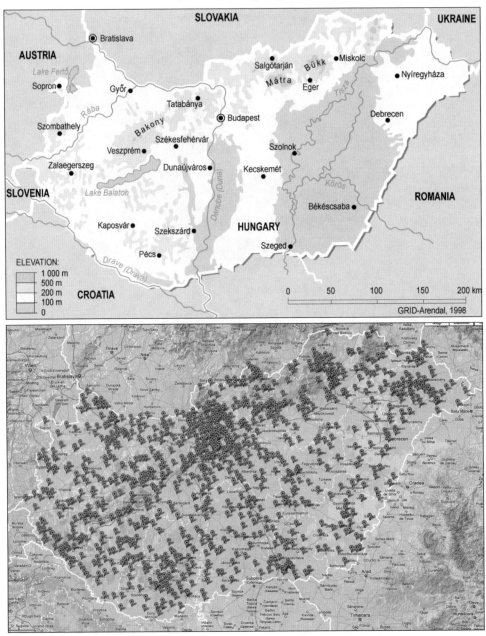

Locations in Hungary where YTL is taught.

Authors

Dave Robinson —www.covenantchapel.com and www.storyofthesoul.org

Dave is the former Area Campus Director for Eastern Europe and Russia for Campus Crusade for Christ International. He served from 1989-2007 with Campus Crusade in the following roles: National Director for Hungary and Yugoslavia, Regional Director and Area Campus Director.

He is also the co-founder and author of Youth at the Threshold of Life, an accredited program and curriculum in Hungarian public schools that not only contains the Gospel of Jesus Christ, but also has had the support of the European Union.

Dave currently serves as Pastor of Covenant Chapel, an Evangelical Presbyterian Church in the Kansas City area. Covenant Chapel is a young, dynamic church committed to its community in Johnson County and south Kansas City, 'City-Reaching' in the USA, and strategic mission partnerships worldwide.

Dave and Karen raised their family (Abbie, Dan and Katie) in Budapest, Hungary where they lived for 18 years. They both continue to serve as Affiliate Staff of Campus Crusade and help lead two ministries, Youth at the Threshold of Life and Story of the Soul (an interactive coffeehouse outreach experience).

Gábor Grész —www.advancingthekingdom.hu

Gábor is the National Director of Campus Crusade for Christ Hungary. He is the co-founder and author of Youth at the Threshold of Life, an accredited program and curriculum in Hungarian public schools that contains the Gospel of Jesus Christ.

Gábor is an ordained Presbyterian minister and graduated in 1991 from the Reformed Theological Seminary of Budapest, Hungary. He is a Teaching Elder in the Rózsakert Baptist Church which he helped plant 20 years ago. He is a well-known Bible teacher and conference speaker in Hungary.

Gábor and his wife, Edina, have served as full-time staff with Campus Crusade since 1992. They live with their three children (Ráhel, Renátó and Gergő) in Budapest, Hungary.

Interactive Internet Resources

www.advancingthekingdom.hu

www.storyofthesoul.org

www.covenantchapel.com

www.outrageouspromise.com